Pass the Virginia Pharmacy Law Exam

A Study Guide for the FSDLE

2nd Edition

By Alexis Long, PharmD. and

Douglas Lipton, JD, BS Pharm.

Copyright © 2015 Alexis Long and Douglas Lipton

All rights reserved.

Table of Contents

Introduction..7
Licensing, Registration and Inspection.................................10
    The Board of Pharmacy..10
    Pharmacist Licensing..12
    Pharmacy Technicians 20
    Pharmacy Physical Standards..23
    Pharmacy Permits...25
    Pharmacy Closings and Transfers 29
    DEA Registration 30
    Drugs and Drug Classifications...33
    Misbranding and Adulteration...37
    Definitions 38
Prescriptions...40
    Prescribing Authority 40
    Prescriptions and Chart Orders..43
    Faxed Prescriptions 51
    Electronic Prescriptions...53
    Intangible Prescription Requirements 55
Dispensing and Distribution 58

Refills and Partial Fills 58

Pharmacy Practice & Dispensing 63

Prescription Transfers...66

Generic Substitution 68

Prescription Labeling..70

Prescription Drug Packaging 71

Pharmacy Access..73

Dispensing of Non-Prescription CV Controlled Substances..............76

Dispensing of Non-Prescription Insulin 77

Dispensing of Non-Prescription Controlled Paraphernalia 77

Dispensing of Non-Prescription Methamphetamine Precursors 79

Dispensing of Non-Prescription Dextromethorphan 80

Prescription Delivery 81

Ordering, Receiving, and Managing Drug Inventory 82

Drug Acquisition 83

Prescription Drug Returns 84

Drug Distribution...86

DEA Form 222 and Schedule II Drug Transfers..86

Drug Disposal/Destruction 91

Inventory & Recordkeeping Requirements 93

Inventories 93

Prescription Recordkeeping..96

Additional Recordkeeping..97

Pharmacy Inspections 100

Prescription Drug Samples 103

Robotic Systems 104

Prescription Monitoring Program ("PMP").......................................105

Theft or Loss of Drugs 106

Maintenance, Detoxification and Treatment of Addiction 108

Hospital & Long-term Care Pharmacy...109

Automated Dispensing Systems 111

Floor Stock 115

Long Term Care Facilities..117

Unit Dose Dispensing Systems...119

Compounding 121

Automated Dispensing Bins 125

Central Fill and Central Processing of Prescriptions.........................126

Stat Drug Boxes and Emergency Drug Kits 132

Stat Drug Boxes 132

EMT Boxes...134

Collaborative Practice Agreements 135

Collaborative Practice Agreements 135

About the Authors 138

Introduction

To the uninitiated, pharmacy law may appear to consist of a diverse conglomeration of federal and state statutes and regulations with significant overlap and no apparent or definitive organization. This introduction is intended to assist the reader in developing a basic understanding of pharmacy law's regulatory framework and the major principles that drive pharmacy law.

The regulatory framework of pharmacy is relatively complex because both federal and state legislative and regulatory bodies are involved. The legislative bodies whose enactments govern pharmacy practice in Virginia are the U.S. Congress and the Virginia General Assembly. The laws passed by both of these legislatures can affect pharmacy practice in Virginia and govern the actions of practicing pharmacists.

The primary regulatory bodies whose actions govern pharmacy practice in Virginia are: the Federal Food & Drug Administration (FDA), the federal Drug Enforcement Administration (DEA), and the Virginia Board of Pharmacy ("Board"). The regulations of the DEA and Virginia Board of Pharmacy make up the vast majority of regulations that govern pharmacists' actions on a daily basis. This is because the Board of Pharmacy is responsible for the regulation of pharmacy practice and the DEA is responsible for assuring compliance with federal controlled substance law.

A cursory review of the major pharmacy legislative acts passed by Congress will assist the reader in developing an understanding of pharmacy laws' primary goals. Having this understanding should help readers remember the law they are learning in this book and increase the their skill in choosing the correct answers to pharmacy law questions.

All readers of this text should already be familiar with the major federal enactments of pharmacy related law. These Acts include: the Pure Food & Drug Act of 1906, the Food, Drug, and Cosmetic Act of 1938, the Durham Humphrey and Kefauver Harris Amendments to the Food, Drug, and Cosmetic Act, and the Federal Controlled Substance Act of 1970.

The Pure Food & Drug Act of 1906 prohibited the shipment of adulterated or misbranded drugs in interstate commerce. Readers familiar with the specific language of the Pure Food & Drug Act will notice that these prohibitions continue to exist in Federal law in the Federal Food, Drug & Cosmetic Act.

Similar language is also found in Virginia's Drug Control Act. The major principles that flow from the Pure Food & Drug Act are that drugs need to meet quality and purity standards and that drugs must be properly labeled as to their contents.

The Federal Food, Drug & Cosmetic Act increased the labeling requirements and implemented the first drug safety requirements. Having realized that some drugs could only be safely used under the supervision of a prescriber, Congress then passed the Durham Humphrey Amendment, which divided drugs into the classes of prescription and non-prescription drugs.

The Kefauver Harris Amendment followed and required (finally) that drugs actually be efficacious. Lastly, Congress passed the Controlled Substances Act (CSA) in 1970. The CSA categorized drugs that were addictive and/or subject to abuse based on the relative risk posed by the drugs and created a closed system of distribution to minimize the risk that these drugs would end up being abused.

Together, these laws assure that drugs in the United States:

- Meet quality and purity standards
- Are both safe and effective
- Are labeled to allow safe use by patients or provide for use only under medical supervision; and
- Are required to flow through appropriately licensed entities to minimize the possibility of drug diversion and abuse.

The vast majority of the laws and regulations that govern pharmacy practice can be tied back to one of the purposes set forth immediately above and the reader should take mental notes throughout the remainder of the text as to what purpose is being served by each specific legal or regulatory requirement. Doing so will likely help the reader retain the knowledge contained in this book and increase the reader's chance of correctly answering questions on the licensing exam. An example of this thinking is as follows:

Question: Why are there specific storage temperature requirements for drugs in a pharmacy?

Answer: To assure the quality and purity of the drug.

Analysis: If a pharmacist were a patient with angina, would the pharmacist want his nitroglycerin stored in a loosely sealed container and left in a high humidity and high temperature environment for an extended period of time? Of course not!

Why: Because the purity and quality of the drug could (and likely would) be negatively affected.

Final introductory thoughts: Pharmacists often become so familiar with the skilled and appropriate use of medications that they tend to overlook one very important characteristic of drugs. To wit: Drugs are NOT safe! Instead, drugs are inherently dangerous and may be fairly characterized as poisons. Drugs are made safe to use by by the multitude of legal requirements placed on the drug industry, pharmacists, prescribers, and others involved in the medication distribution chain.

For instance, most people would consider aspirin 325 mg USP tablets to be a safe product. Aspirin has been on the market for many years and most adults have taken this medication with good results.

Now, imagine the removal of all of the regulatory controls placed on this product. Does the removal of warnings from the aspirin's label all of a sudden make it safe for use in a 10 year child who has a high fever from chicken pox or for a patient who also takes warfarin?

Would acetaminophen 325 mg USP tablets be safe for consumption if each tablet contained 5,000 mg instead of 325 mg? Would rifampin have no effect on the metabolism of warfarin if the patient were able to purchase both drugs without a prescription? The answer to these questions is obviously a resounding NO. Almost all drugs, even aspirin, are inherently dangerous.

The vast majority of the pharmacy laws and regulations you will be studying in this book reflect the government's attempts to put into place the controls necessary to make the use of inherently dangerous drugs safe. Try to keep this concept in mind as you read this text and you will begin to see the entire puzzle instead of just the pieces. Good luck!

Licensing, Registration and Inspection

As you read through the questions below, be sure to quiz yourself by attempting to answer the question in your mind before reading the answer. It's important to train your brain in active recall so that details of the law will come back to you more easily when you are actually taking the exam.

According to guidelines published on the Virginia Board of Pharmacy's web site, 24% of the exam covers licensing, registration and inspection.

As you read through this and following sections, be sure to keep in mind the most important aspects of the law. As a practicing pharmacist, you will find licensing regulations extremely important. That is covered in this section.

Later sections cover other important material. You will need a solid understanding of inventory management. You will also need a firm grasp of the various laws regulating prescriptions. How do you know a prescription is valid? Finally, be sure to carefully study the laws regarding drug transfers, such as selling, borrowing, dispensing, and disposing of CII-V drugs. As a pharmacist, you will have ultimate responsibility for the controlled substances at your site of practice.

The Board of Pharmacy

What governmental entity regulates the practice of pharmacy in Virginia?

The Virginia Board of Pharmacy ("Board").

What are the powers and duties of the Board?

The Board regulates the practice of pharmacy and the manufacturing, dispensing, selling, distributing, processing, compounding, and disposal of drugs and devices in Virginia. These duties include the regulation of the character and quality of drugs.

What else is the Board of Pharmacy responsible for regulating?

- The maintenance of the quality, quantity, integrity, safety and efficacy of drugs and devices distributed, dispensed or administered in Virginia.
- The maintenance of complete records of controlled substances.
- The assurance of compliance with prescribed instructions relating to drug quantity, quality and directions for use.
- Controlling factors contributing to the abuse of legitimately obtained drugs.
- Controls and safeguards against the diversion of drugs or devices.
- The promotion of scientific or technical advances in the practice of pharmacy.
- The impact of pharmacy costs to the public.
- The integrity and public confidence in the profession of pharmacy and the improvement in the delivery of pharmaceutical services.

The Board also has authority to implement a "pedigree system" to apply to certain schedules or drugs that are more subject to counterfeiting. What is a "pedigree"?

"Pedigree" means a paper document or electronic file recording each distribution of a controlled substance. It includes sale by a pharmaceutical manufacturer through acquisition and sale by any wholesale distributor until sale to a pharmacy or other person dispensing or administering the controlled substance.

Pharmacist Licensing

What do you need to do to obtain a pharmacist's license in Virginia?

- Graduate from an ACPE approved school of pharmacy – there are different rules for foreign-trained pharmacists
- Obtain 1500 hours of practical experience as a pharmacy intern
- Obtain a passing score on the NAPLEX Exam
- Obtain a passing score on the Virginia Federal and State Drug Law Exam
- Be of good moral character and over the age of 18

How do you obtain the 1500 hours of practical experience required in Virginia?

All of your practical experience must be gained in the United States after receiving your intern license.

Virginia allows you to obtain all of your practical experience through your ACPE accredited school of pharmacy.

You can gain hours outside of your school's curriculum but those hours must occur after you have completed two semesters of pharmacy school.

Who is a pharmacy intern?

A pharmacy intern is a student who is currently enrolled in or a graduate of an approved school of pharmacy who is registered with the Board for the purpose of gaining the practical experience required to apply for licensure as a pharmacist.

Are there any other requirements for practical experience gained outside of your ACPE accredited school of pharmacy?

Yes. The hours cannot exceed 50 hours per week and must also include a minimum average of 20 hours per week for any month wherein practical experience hours are claimed.

Are there any requirements of the person who is supervising an intern who is in the process of acquiring intern hours?

Yes. The intern must be supervised by a pharmacist who has a current and unrestricted license to practice pharmacy. The supervising pharmacist is required to assume full responsibility for the supervision, training, and conduct of the intern.

How many interns can a pharmacist supervise at one time?

Virginia law no longer specifies a limit. A pharmacist is allowed to supervise a maximum of 4 pharmacy technicians and interns who are acting as pharmacy technicians are included in that maximum. A pharmacist can supervise a pharmacy intern in addition to the 4 technicians provided the intern is gaining practical experience and is not engaged in technician functions.

Does "supervision" have a specific meaning in Virginia pharmacy law? Can a pharmacist supervise over the phone; leave written instructions; or use any kind of electronic monitoring?

Virginia law defines supervision and it must be done in person. The pharmacist must be physically present and available for immediate oral communication.

Is "personal supervision" different than supervision?

Yes. The pharmacist must be physically present and directly control the service or act. Being available for oral communication is not sufficient.

What happens if an applicant fails the NAPLEX portion of the pharmacy licensing exam?

The applicant may retake the exam.

What happens if an applicant fails the NAPLEX portion of the exam multiple times?

If an applicant fails the exam three times, he will have to get an additional 1,000 hours of practical experience before being allowed to retake the exam.

What happens if an applicant fails the Virginia Federal and State Drug Law Exam?

The applicant will have to wait 30 days to retake the exam.

When will your Virginia pharmacist's license expire?

Annually on December 31st of each year.

Does the date of initial licensure change the expiration date for the first year?

It can. A newly licensed pharmacist who received his license on or after October 1st will not need to renew his license until December 31st of the following year.

How do you renew your pharmacist's license?

- Submit a completed renewal form prior to December 31st
- Pay the annual renewal fee; currently $90.00
- Submit a statement of compliance with the continuing education requirements

What do you have to do if you move and have a new address?

You have to inform of the Board of your current address within 14 days. You can do this in writing or electronically via the Board's online web based application.

How many hours of continuing education (CE) are required to renew your license?

You need to obtain 15 contact hours of CE each calendar year, which is the equivalent of 1.5 Continuing Education Units (CEUs).

Are you required to complete CE prior to your first license renewal?

It depends on when you received your license. You are not required to obtain CE for your first license renewal unless you were initially licensed on or after October 1st of that year.

For instance, if you were licensed on July 1, 2015, you would not need to complete CE prior to renewing your license on December 31, 2015. But, if you were first licensed on October 1, 2015 and did not have to renew your license until December 31, 2016, you would have to meet the CE requirements prior to renewing your license in 2016.

Can you carry extra hours of CE over to the following year?

No. They do not carry over.

What types of CE programs are acceptable to meet Virgina's requirements?

- CE programs approved by the American Council on Pharmacy

Education (ACPE)
- Category 1 Continuing Medical Education (CME) that is focused on pharmacy, pharmacology, or drug therapy
- Any other program specifically approved by the Virginia Board of Pharmacy ("Board")

How long are you required to keep records of your completion of CE?

Two years following the renewal of your license. You are responsible for maintaining these records in your files and providing them to the Board upon request.

Can CE earned for a license in another state be used to meet Virginia's CE requirements?

Yes, as long as it meets the requirements for Virginia CE as detailed above.

Can a pharmacist get an exemption from the CE requirements?

Yes, but such exemptions are rarely granted and only when there were circumstances outside of the pharmacist's control.

Can the Board grant a pharmacist an extension to fulfill the CE requirements?

Yes. The Board can give a pharmacist a one-year extension to fulfill the CE requirements based on the written request of the pharmacist.

Does an extension affect the pharmacist's requirement to get CE the following year?

No. The pharmacist is responsible for both the CE he missed and the CE he must get for the new year.

What if you do not renew your license prior to the December 31st expiration date?

You can still renew your license within one year of its expiration by:
- Submitting a completed renewal form
- Paying the annual renewal fee
- Submitting a statement of compliance with the continuing education requirements, and
- Paying a late fee

Does renewing the expired license the following year change the CE requirements?

No. You are still responsible for the previous year's and the current year's CE.

What if you waited more than a year to renew your license?

Your license will be considered "inactive" and you will have to apply for reinstatement of the license.

How do you apply for reinstatement of your license?

- Submit an application for reinstatement
- Pay the renewal fee
- Pay the reinstatement fee
- Submit documentation of completion of CE

How much CE is required to reinstate a license that was inactive?

The same amount that the pharmacist would have needed to renew the license each year. For instance: if the pharmacist's license was inactive for three years, she would need to obtain 45 hours of CE or 4.5 CEUs to get her license reinstated.

Is there a limit on the amount of CE the Board will require for reinstatement of an inactive license?

Yes. The maximum number of hours of CE that will be required is 60.

Does the Board of Pharmacy have to grant reinstatement of a license that has been inactive for more than a year?

No. The Board has discretion to grant or deny reinstatement. The executive director of the Board can grant reinstatement if no grounds exist to deny reinstatement.

Are there any additional requirements for a pharmacist whose license was inactive for more than five years?

Yes. The pharmacist will need to produce proof of practice in another state within the last 5 years or have obtained 160 hours of practical experience as a Virginia Pharmacy Intern within the previous 6 months. The pharmacist will also need to have completed the required 60 hours of CE and will have to retake the Virginia Federal and State Drug Law Exam.

Is a pharmacist with an inactive licensed required to continue completing CE every year?

No, but the pharmacist will not be able to convert his license to active status until he completes the equivalent hours of CE for the inactive period up to the 60 hour maximum.

Who can sanction a pharmacist and suspend or revoke a pharmacist's license?

The Board of Pharmacy.

What sanctions, in addition to suspension or revocation of a pharmacist's license, are available to the Board?

- Reprimand
- Monetary penalty
- Probation
- Imposition of terms on the pharmacist's license (e.g. additional CE or restricted practice)

What are the grounds for sanctions, suspension, or revocation of a pharmacist's license?

- Has been negligent in the practice of pharmacy or another permitted activity
- Has engaged in unprofessional conduct
- Is incompetent to practice because of a physical or mental condition
- Is unsafe to practice because of drug or alcohol use
- Has engaged in or attempted fraudulent or deceitful conduct related to pharmacy practice
- Has engaged in activities beyond the scope of his license
- Has allowed unlicensed person to engage in activities that require a license or permit
- Has violated or cooperated with others in violating laws or regulations governing the practice of pharmacy
- Has had a license, permit, or registration issued by the DEA or another federal agency denied, suspended, or revoked

- Has engaged in the theft or diversion of controlled substances
- Has violated any federal or state drug law
- Has had a license related to the practice of pharmacy suspended, revoked, or denied in another state
- Has been convicted of a felony
- Has been convicted of misdemeanor involving moral turpitude (lying, cheating, or stealing offenses; e.g. giving a false police report or shoplifting)
- Has issued or published deceptive or fraudulent statements related to a professional service regulated by the Board
- Has practiced in a manner that was dangerous to the health and welfare of the public
- Has failed to comply with CE requirements

What if a pharmacist's licensed in suspended in another state solely due to the pharmacist's failure to renew the license?

The Board will not sanction the pharmacist's Virginia license.

What constitutes "unprofessional conduct" in Virginia?

- Failing to comply with Virginia's patient health record confidentiality and disclosure laws
- Willfully or negligently breaching patient confidentiality in violation of Virginia law
- Violating the confidentiality provisions of the Prescription Monitoring Program
- Engaging in disruptive or abusive behavior in a healthcare setting that interferes with patient care or could negatively affect the quality of patient care
- Engaging in an inappropriate relationship with a patient that constitutes a boundary violation
- Failing to maintain adequate safeguards against drug diversion
- Failing to respond to a known dispensing error in a manner that protects the health of the patient

- Delegating a pharmacy practice task to a person who is not adequately trained
- Failure by the PIC to ensure that all pharmacy personnel are currently licensed
- Failing to exercise professional judgment in determining whether a prescription meets all legal requirements before dispensing it

Does Virginia recognize a patient's right to privacy of his confidential health records and prohibit the disclosure of such records without the patient's consent?

Yes.

Are pharmacists allowed to provide patient information to other healthcare providers and insurance companies to provide care to a patient?

Yes.

Does a pharmacy have to provide a patient with his records if he requests them?

Yes.

Is a pharmacist allowed to provide a patient's prescription records to a court in response to a lawfully issued subpoena duces tecum (subpoena for records)?

Yes. But the pharmacist needs to carefully read and follow the directions on the subpoena because the patient is allowed to move to have the subpoena quashed (dismissed). A pharmacist should consult his pharmacy's legal counsel before providing records in response to a subpoena.

Is a pharmacist always entitled to a hearing prior to the suspension of his license?

No. A pharmacist's license can be immediately suspended if he presents a danger to the public health or safety. A hearing will be scheduled within a reasonable time.

What other circumstances can result in a pharmacist's license being immediately suspended without a hearing by the Director of the Board of Health Professions?

- The pharmacist is convicted of a felony.
- The pharmacist is adjudicated incapacitated (not competent) by a court.
- The pharmacist has his license to practice in another jurisdiction suspended or revoked.

What if the felony conviction is not final?

The director can decline to suspend the license if there is a likelihood of injury to the public if the pharmacist's services are not available. This would apply if a pharmacist owns his own pharmacy in a small town and pharmacy services would be made unavailable to his patients.

If a pharmacist's license is suspended, how does he apply for reinstatement?

He can bring counsel and witnesses to the Board hearing and will need ¾ of the Board members at the hearing to vote for reinstatement. The Board may also reinstate only upon terms or conditions as it deems appropriate.

Pharmacy Technicians

What is a pharmacy technician?

A person who is registered with the Board to assist a pharmacist under the pharmacist's supervision.

How does a person to obtain registration as a pharmacy technician?

A technician must hold a current certification by the Pharmacy Technician Certification Board (PTCB) OR complete an approved training program, pass the Virginia technician exam, complete the application, and pay the licensing fee.

Does a technician who only works in a free clinic have to be registered?

Yes. The Board can issue a limited-use registration (free clinic only). The Board will waive the initial registration fee and first examination fee for this type of registration. If the technician wants to switch to an unlimited registration, all that is required is payment of the current renewal fee.

Can unregistered technicians work as pharmacy technicians while

enrolled in a training program to become registered?

Yes, as long as they are being directly monitored by a pharmacist.

How long can a technician trainee work before obtaining his registration?

9 months.

When does a technician need to renew his or her registration?

Before December 31st each year. A technician who is newly licensed on July 1st or later doesn't need to renew his registration until December 31st of the following year.

Are pharmacy technicians required to complete CE every year?

Yes. Technicians are required to obtain 5 hours of CE or 0.5 CEUs every year. It is possible to get a 1 year extension with a written request – but the technician would still need to complete the full amount of CE.

What if a technician renews his or her registration late?

Within the first year, the technician must pay a late fee, the renewal fee, complete the renewal form, and certify his completion of the required CE.

After 1 year, the technician pays a reinstatement fee, a renewal fee, completes the application for reinstatement and certifies his completion of CE.

After 5 or more years, the technician will need to apply for recertification. The same requirements will apply as for initial registration of the technician.

How long is a technician required keep her records of completion of CE?

Two years following renewal. The technician, not the employer, is required to maintain these records.

How many technicians can a pharmacist supervise at one time?

Four. This includes technicians, technician trainees, and pharmacy interns who are performing pharmacy technician activities.

What acts are restricted to pharmacy technicians?

- Entering prescription information and drug history information into a data system or other record keeping system

- Preparing prescription labels and patient information
- Removing drugs to be dispensed from inventory
- Counting, measuring and compounding drugs to be dispensed
- Packaging and labeling drugs to be dispensed, including repackaging
- Stocking and loading automated dispensing devices or other devices that are used in the dispensing process
- Accepting refill authorization from a prescriber provided there are no changes from the original prescription
- Performing any act restricted to pharmacy technicians by the Board's regulations.

Can "acts restricted to pharmacy technicians" be completed by pharmacists or pharmacy interns?

Yes

When can a pharmacy technician at a nuclear pharmacy accept oral prescriptions?

A technician at a nuclear pharmacy can accept oral prescriptions for diagnostic non-patient specific radiopharmaceuticals.

Can a technician compound extemporaneous preparations?

Yes, but a pharmacist must personally supervise the preparation.

What documents must be maintained by a pharmacy that employs technicians?

- A site-specific training program and manual
- Documentation of completion of this training for each technician, which must be kept for 2 years after the technician leaves the employer
- For technician trainees, proof that they are enrolled in an approved training program.

Pharmacy Physical Standards

What are the physical requirements for a Virginia licensed

prescription department?

- It must be at least 240 square feet; not including the patient waiting area or the area used for counseling, devices, cosmetics, and proprietary medicines.
- Rest rooms and stock rooms must not be accessed through the prescription area. If there is a restroom within the prescription area, it must be for pharmacy personnel only.
- It must have a sink with hot and cold running water.
- There must be a refrigerator with a monitoring thermometer for drugs that require cold storage temperatures if such drugs are stocked in the pharmacy.
- It must be well lighted, well ventilated, and the temperature must meet USP standards for drug storage.

What does "storage temperature" mean?

The temperatures required for the safe storage of drugs as specified in the drugs' monographs.

What temperature ranges are specified in the Board's regulations?

- Freezer temperature = -20 to -10C (-4 to 14F)
- Refrigerator temperature = 2-8C (36-46F)
- Cold = <8C (46F)
- Cool = 8-15C (46-59F)
- Room temperature = work area temperature
- Controlled room temperature = 20-25C (68-77F)
- Warm = 30-40C (86-104F)
- Excessive heat = >40C (104F)
- Protection from freezing – means that freezing the drug subjects it to a change in potency.
- Remember: Fahrenheit Temperature = (1.8 x Celsius Temperature) + 32

Can you use a trailer as a pharmacy?

No, a pharmacy must be located in a permanent and secure structure.

What minimum equipment is required for a pharmacy?

- A current dispensing information reference source
- Either an electronic scale or a set of prescription balances (sensitive to 15 milligrams) and weights if the dispensing activities require weighing
- Other equipment, supplies, and references consistent with the pharmacy's scope of practice and with public safety

Are pharmacies required to have a security system?

Yes.

What is an exception to the pharmacy security system requirement?

Pharmacies that are open 24 hours a day, 7 days a week, and that are always staffed by a pharmacist do not have to have a security system. A 24 hour pharmacy would need to install a security system before it could change its hours to less than those of a 24 hour pharmacy.

What are the requirements for the pharmacy security system's device(s)?

- It must be a "generally accepted" device for the industry, such as sound, microwave, photoelectric, or ultrasonic.
- It must be in working order and have a backup power supply.
- It must be able to send an alarm even if the communication line is not working (e.g. it must alarm if the communication line is cut).
- It must fully protect the prescription area and detect any type of breaking.

Who may have the code to access the alarm system?

Pharmacists working at the pharmacy who have been authorized by the pharmacist in charge ("PIC") to have the access code.

When must the security system be activated?

Whenever the prescription department is closed for business.

What are the prescription department enclosure requirements?

- It be constructed so that it protects against unauthorized entry and theft of controlled substances at all times, whether a pharmacist is on duty or not.

- The prescription department enclosure must be locked and alarmed whenever a pharmacist is not on duty.
- It must be capable of being locked when the on duty pharmacist is not in the prescription department.

Pharmacy Permits

Who obtains a permit from the Board of Pharmacy to conduct (operate) a pharmacy in Virginia?

The Pharmacist-In-Charge (PIC) who will be in actual charge of the practice of pharmacy at the location on the application. The permit will not be issued to a business entity.

What has to be on the application for the permit to operate a pharmacy?

- The pharmacy's corporate name and trade name
- Any pharmacists in addition to the PIC who will be practicing at the pharmacy
- The hours the pharmacy will be open
- The pharmacy owner, if someone other than the PIC
- The type of ownership (corporation, partnership) and names of the partners, directors, or officers

Is it possible to get a special or limited-use pharmacy permit?

Yes. The Board has the discretion to issue a special or limited-use permit. The applicant would need to list the regulatory requirements he wants waived and why. The pharmacy must also maintain a policy and procedure manual outlining the type of operation, hours, method of documenting continuing pharmacist control, and schedules of drugs maintained.

Can a pharmacist be the PIC of more than one pharmacy?

Yes. A pharmacist may be the PIC of a maximum of 2 pharmacies.

What is the next step in the process after the application for the permit to operate a pharmacy is submitted?

The location of the new pharmacy must be inspected by an agent of the Board before the pharmacy permit can be issued.

If the pharmacy permit application indicates a requested inspection date, will the Board honor the request for the inspection to occur on that specific date?

Yes, as long as the application provides the Board with 14 days notice prior to the requested inspection date.

What if the requested inspection date is less than 14 days from the date the application is submitted?

The Board may adjust to the date to provide for at least 14 days to schedule the inspection.

What requirements will the new pharmacy have to meet for the inspector to approve the issuance of a pharmacy permit?

- All applicable physical standards (e.g. at least 240 square feet)
- The sanitary condition standards
- The required minimum equipment and resource standards
- The security system standards
- The prescription department enclosure and access standards

What will happen if the inspector does not approve the pharmacy or if the applicant is not ready by the inspection date?

The applicant will have to pay a re-inspection fee and the pharmacy will have to be re-inspected. If the applicant provides the inspector or Board with 24 hours advance notice that he is not ready for the inspection, the inspection will be rescheduled and he will not have to pay the additional re-inspection fee.

Before the inspection, can drugs be stocked in the pharmacy?

No. Drugs cannot be moved into a new location for an existing pharmacy either. If you don't have a permit, you can't stock drugs.

When can the PIC begin to stock the new pharmacy with drugs?

After passing the inspection and no sooner than 14 days prior to the designated opening date.

How are the safety and integrity of the drugs ensured prior to the opening of the pharmacy?

A pharmacist has to be present at the pharmacy on a daily basis.

What if the opening date for the pharmacy changes?

The pharmacist has to notify the Board and continue to be on site on a daily basis.

How often does a pharmacy permit have to be renewed?

Annually.

Is the pharmacy required to display its permit?

Yes, it must be displayed prominently.

Under what circumstances does the PIC need to turn in the pharmacy permit and make a new application?

If there is any change in ownership of the pharmacy, such as a change in partnership composition or acquisition.

What happens if the PIC leaves her position with the pharmacy?

The PIC must immediately surrender the pharmacy permit to the Board. Remember, the permit is issued to the PIC and not to the pharmacy.

How long can a PIC be absent for a scheduled leave before the pharmacy has to notify the Board and designate a new PIC?

The PIC may be absent for up to 30 days for a scheduled leave of absence. If she is gone for more than 30 days, the pharmacy will need to notify the Board and designate a new PIC.

What if the PIC is has an unscheduled absence?

If the PIC has a 15 day unscheduled absence and no known return date within the next 15 days, the Board must be notified and a new PIC designated.

How will the pharmacy get a new permit?

The incoming PIC will apply for the new permit.

What does a new PIC have to do when taking over responsibility for a pharmacy?

Inventory all Schedule I, II, III, IV and V drugs on the day he or she becomes PIC. The inventory must be completed before the pharmacy opens for business that day.

When the PIC leaves, how long does the pharmacy have to designate a new PIC?

14 days.

Can a pharmacy keep operating if it fails to designate a new PIC within 14 days after the old PIC leaves?

No. It is not even allowed to maintain a stock of prescription drugs unless it requests an extension from the Board of the time allowed to designate a new PIC.

Who can grant a pharmacy an extension of the time allowed to obtain a new PIC?

The executive director of the Board can give the pharmacy an additional 14 days to designate a PIC for good cause shown. But, the extension request has to be received prior to the original deadline.

If the pharmacy does not have a PIC and receives a notice from the Board that it does not have a valid permit, what is the pharmacy required to do?

Dispose properly of all Schedule II through VI drugs and devices on the premises within fifteen days.

What if the pharmacy fails to do dispose of the drugs?

The Board will seize all Schedule II through VI drugs and devices still on the premises and notify the owner.

Can the pharmacy's owner get the drugs back?

Yes. The owner can claim the drugs by paying storage costs and providing for proper disposition of the drugs.

How long does the owner have to claim the drugs?

Six months. If the drugs have not been claimed by then, the drugs may be destroyed.

If the pharmacy is being sold, can the pharmacy permit be transferred to the new owners?

No, the permit is nontransferable and must be returned to the Board.

Does the Board need to be notified if the pharmacy is changing locations, making changes to a previously approved security system, or if structural changes are being made to the pharmacy?

Yes. The pharmacy will need to be inspected by an agent of the Board and the Board needs to be given 14 days notice before the inspection is scheduled. A new location will need to be inspected before any drugs can be stocked there.

What must be done if the hours of operation of the pharmacy change?

If the change is expected to last more than a week, the change must be reported in writing to the Board and the pharmacy must post a conspicuous notice 14 days before the change to inform the pharmacy's patients.

Pharmacy Closings and Transfers

What do you need to do if you want to close your pharmacy?

If it will be closed for more than 1 week, the pharmacy must post a notice 30 days prior to closing or mail a notice 14 days prior to closing to every patient with available refills.

What must be included in the notice?

The notice must include the date of closing and name of the pharmacy that records will be transferred to unless patients indicate a preference to the contrary.

If there is a change in pharmacy ownership, which records must be transferred?

The last two years of prescription dispensing records and patient records.

What happens if a pharmacy refuses to process a request for prescription dispensing records or other records tendered in accordance with law?

It constitutes a closing.

When a pharmacy is closing, does the Board need to be notified?

Yes, the pharmacy must report how it intends to dispose of all CII-VI drugs, prescription dispensing and patient records. This includes the name and address of any licensee who will receive the drugs and records, and the date of transfer.

The pharmacy is going to change ownership. Does the Board need to be notified?

The pharmacy must notify the Board 14 days prior to the change in ownership, and transfer the preceding two years' prescription and dispensing records. Remember, the PIC will have to get a new permit.

One pharmacy is being acquired by another. Do current patients need to be notified?

Only if prescription records are going to be used for something other than continuity of pharmacy services at substantially the same level. If so, written notice must be given 14 days prior to the acquisition.

DEA Registration

Are pharmacies required to obtain a DEA registration (DEA number)?

Yes. A DEA registration is necessary to possess Federal controlled substances (CI-CV) drugs. A pharmacy would not need a DEA registration if it were only going to possess and dispense CVI medications.

What form does a pharmacy complete to obtain a DEA registration?

DEA Form 224 for the initial registration and DEA 224a for renewal of the registration.

When will the initial registration expire?

It will expire in 28 to 39 months. The DEA varies the initial expiration dates so it can assign new registrants to a cohort for renewal. This prevents all of the registrations from having to be renewed at the same time.

After the initial registration is renewed, how often does a pharmacy need to renew its registration with the DEA?

Every 3 years. Each renewed registration will have a 3 year expiration date.

Do agents of the registrant (pharmacists) need to be separately registered?

No. In fact, the registrant can authorize his agent(s) to order CII drugs, complete DEA 222 forms, and to renew his DEA registration by completion of a Power of Attorney. Regular employees of a pharmacy do not need to be registered either.

If a pharmacy, manufacturer, or other entity has more than one place of business, how many DEA registrations do they need?

One for each place of business or practice location.

How often does a manufacturer need to re-register with the DEA?

Every year.

If a pharmacist owns two independent pharmacies at different locations, does the pharmacist have to obtain two separate DEA registration, one for each pharmacy?

Yes. Each location must have its own DEA registration.

What are the separate business activities that each require their own DEA registration number?

- Manufacturing
- Distributing
- Reverse distributing
- Dispensing
- Research (CI drugs)
- Research (CII-V drugs)
- Narcotic treatment (including compounder)
- Importing
- Exporting
- Chemical analysis

Can a pharmacy engage in the other business activities using its DEA registration to dispense medications?

No. A pharmacy's DEA registration allows it to possess and dispense CII-CV medications. It would need a different DEA registration to engage in the other activities.

Are there any organizations that are exempt from paying DEA registration fees (but not exempt from getting the appropriate DEA registration)?

Yes. Facilities operated by a United States agency (including the U.S. Army, Navy, Marine Corps., Air Force, and Coast Guard), or by any state, are exempt from paying fees.

A facility wants to handle CI drugs for research purposes. The facility already has a DEA number. What else is the facility required to do?

Apply for a modified DEA registration by submitting 3 copies of the research protocol. There is no fee for modification and it is handled just like a regular registration application.

When is a registrant's DEA registration considered terminated?

If the registrant dies, if the business ceases legal existence, if the registrant surrenders his registration to the DEA, or if the person discontinues his business or professional practice.

If a pharmacy ceases business, what are its responsibilities to the DEA?

Notify the DEA

Return the certificate of registration and unexecuted order forms (DEA 222 Forms)

Dispose of Federal controlled substances properly

Can a pharmacy transfer its registration to the new owner(s) after being acquired?

Yes. The registrant must submit a written request to the Deputy Assistant Administrator, Office of Diversion Control in Washington, DC.

Can a DEA registrant discontinue business and transfer the business to another registrant?

Yes. The transferor has to provide (in person or via certified mail return receipt requested) the Special Agent in Charge of his area a notice at least 14 days prior to the date of the proposed transfer.

What must be included in the transfer notice request?

- The names, addresses, DEA numbers, and authorized business activities of both the transferring and receiving registrants

- Where business will be conducted and the new address if it is different from where the transferring business was located
- The date the transfer of controlled substances will occur
- Any quota the transferor had to manufacture or procure CI or CII drugs.

Will the pharmacy receive any special paperwork from the Special Agent in Charge authorizing the transfer?

No. If the date the of the transfer arrives and the pharmacy hasn't been informed that it cannot occur, the transfer may take place.

What must be done on the date of transfer?

- A complete inventory of all CI-CV controlled substances (both transferor and transferee need to keep a copy of this inventory)
- Use a DEA 222 order form if transferring CI-CII substances
- All required records of the transferor that relate to the controlled substances must be transferred to the transferee.
- Registrants that are required to file reports (e.g., registrants that routinely destroy controlled substances) must file a final report.

What else does the outgoing PIC have to do?

Return the pharmacy permit to the Board immediately.

Which entities are required to register with the Federal Food & Drug Administration (FDA)?

Manufacturers, compounders and distributors. Pharmacies are not required to register with the FDA.

Drugs and Drug Classifications

What is a drug?

An article intended for use in the diagnosis, mitigation, treatment, or prevention of disease in humans or animals. An article, other than food, that is intended to affect the structure of function of the body is also a drug for purposes of pharmacy law.

A "drug" is also an article recognized in which publications?

- The official United States Pharmacopoeia National Formulary (USP-NF)
- The official Homeopathic Pharmacopoeia of the United States
- A supplement to one of these pharmacopoeia

Is either alcohol or tobacco a drug for purposes of pharmacy law?

No.

What is a "prescription drug?"

A drug that Federal law or regulations prohibits from being dispensed without a prescription. The definition includes finished dosage forms and active ingredients.

How does the FDA decide whether a drug will be an OTC product or prescription drug?

A drug will require a prescription if the manufacturer cannot write adequate directions for use by a layperson, the drug cannot be used safely without medical supervision by a licensed prescriber, or if it contains an addictive substance that is subject to abuse.

Are the labeling requirements different for RX and OTC drugs?

Yes. The requirements for OTC drugs are much more in depth because these drugs are not used under the supervision of a practitioner.

What is a "controlled substance" under Federal law?

A controlled substance under Federal law is any drug that has been classified as a Schedule I, II, III, IV or V drug by the Federal government.

How are the drug Schedules abbreviated?

By the use of a capital letter "C" and roman numerals.

- Schedule I = CI
- Schedule II = CII

- Schedule III = CIII
- Schedule IV = CIV

Is Virginia's definition of "controlled substance" the same as the Federal law definition?

No. Virginia's definition of "controlled substance" includes the same drugs as the Federal definition but also includes any other drug that requires a prescription.

For the remainder of this book, the phrase "controlled substances" will refer to the Virginia definition and "Federal controlled substances" will be used any time the Federal definition applies.

Does Virginia assign these other drugs to a Virginia only schedule?

Yes. Virginia places these drugs in Schedule VI (CVI). This is a schedule that does not exist in Federal law.

What Federal official assigns drugs to the Federal Schedules?

The United States Attorney General.

What factors does the U.S. Attorney General consider when adding or removing a drug from Schedules I-V?

- Its actual or relative potential for abuse
- Scientific evidence of its pharmacological effect, if known
- The state of current scientific knowledge regarding the drug
- Its history and current pattern of abuse
- The scope, duration, and significance of abuse
- What if any, risk there is to the public health
- Its potential to produce psychic or physiological dependence
- Whether the substance is an immediate precursor of a drug that is already scheduled

Can the Virginia Board of Pharmacy schedule or de-schedule drugs under state law?

Yes.

What factors does Virginia consider when scheduling drugs?

The same ones the U.S. Attorney General considers.

What findings by the Board will result in its placing a drug in Schedule I?

- The drug has a high potential for abuse; and
- No accepted medical use in treatment in the United States or lacks accepted safety for use in treatment under medical supervision.
- What findings by the Board will result in its placing a drug in Schedule II?
- The drug has a high potential for abuse;
- A currently accepted medical use in treatment in the United States, or currently accepted medical use with severe restrictions; and
- It's abuse may lead to severe psychic or physical dependence.

What findings by the Board will result in its placing a drug in Schedule III?

- The drug has less potential for abuse than the drugs listed in Schedules I and II
- It has a currently accepted use for medical treatment in the United States
- Its abuse may lead to moderate or low physical dependence or high psychological dependence

What findings by the Board will result in its placing a drug in Schedule IV?

- The drug has a low potential for abuse relative to drugs in Schedule III
- It has a currently accepted use for medical treatment in the United States
- Its abuse may lead to limited physical dependence or psychological dependence relative to the substances in Schedule III

What findings by the Board will result in its placing a drug in Schedule V?

- The drug has a low potential for abuse relative to the controlled substances listed in Schedule IV
- It has a currently accepted use for medical treatment in the United States

- It has limited physical or psychological dependence liability compared to controlled substances listed in Schedule IV

Test practice pointer: The lower the schedule, the more addictive or abusable the drug. Schedule I is the only schedule whose drug/substances do not have a medically accepted use.

What about Virginia's "Schedule VI" classification?

Virginia places the following drugs and devices in Schedule VI:

- Every drug or device not included in Schedules I-V that are only safe for use under the supervision of a licensed practitioner.
- Any drug or device not included in Schedules I-V that Federal law requires be labeled with "Rx Only" or cautionary labeling such as "Federal Law Restricts This Drug To Use By Or On The Order Of A _____." The blank may be filled in with "Physician," "Dentist," "Veterinarian" or other licensed practitioner.

The Board may also designate any compound exempted from Schedules III, IV, or V as Schedule VI.

Are any devices included in Schedule VI?

Yes, devices are included in CVI if they are considered safe for use only under the supervision of a licensed practitioner (e.g. an insulin pump).

If the Virginia Board of Pharmacy wanted to regulate a drug more strictly than Federal law does (for example, place Ambien in Schedule II instead of Schedule IV), are they allowed to do so?

Yes.

Misbranding and Adulteration

The Federal Food, Drug, & Cosmetic Act is primarily focused on ensuring that drugs are safe and effective. Almost all violations of the Federal Food, Drug, & Cosmetic Act will be either misbranding or adulteration or both. Virginia laws on misbranding and adulteration are almost identical to the Federal laws in this area.

To get a firm understanding of the concepts of misbranding and adulteration, the reader should think of all drugs, both OTC and RX, as being hazardous substances. This is easy to conceptualize if you imagine the possible consequences (Reye's Syndrome) of giving aspirin to an 8 year old child who has a fever from chickenpox. Even though aspirin is safely used by millions of people every day, it can be very hazardous.

The misbranding laws require specific labeling for OTC products to require adequate directions for use; warnings against use under certain conditions (such as the aspirin example above) or by children when the use may be dangerous; dosage directions; duration of use directions; and such other labeling as is necessary to protect the consumer. The failure of an OTC product to bear the required "labeling" will result in the product's being "misbranded" in violation of the law. The labeling for prescription products are different because these products are prohibited from being dispensed except under the supervision of a practitioner licensed to prescribe the substances. The labeling of both RX and OTC products are prohibited from containing false or misleading information. Adulteration laws focus on assuring the strength, quality, and purity of drugs.

Definitions

What is a "label?"

The written, printed or graphic matter on a drug's immediate container. If something is required to be on the label, it must be visible on or through the outside container.

What is "labeling?"

The drug label and any additional materials accompanying the drug. The additional materials could be a package insert, a patient information sheet or leaflet, or any other materials that accompany the medication.

Describe situations in which a drug would be considered adulterated.

- The drug is contaminated (contains "any filthy, puid, or decomposed substance").
- The drug or its container contains a harmful substance.
- The drug contains an unsafe color additive.
- The facilities used to make, pack, or hold the drug do not conform to cGMP (current good manufacturing practices).

- The drug was subjected (manufactured, stored, etc.) to insanitary conditions that may have resulted in its becoming contaminated or harmful.
- It doesn't actually contain the strength, quality, or purity of drug that it claims to contain. [practice tip: it is also misbranded because its label is false or misleading]
- It is a drug listed in a compendium (USP) and it does not meet the compendium's requirements and does not plainly state on its label that it differs from the compendium's requirements.
- It is mixed or packed with something that reduces its quality or strength.

Describe situations in which a drug would be considered misbranded.

- Its labeling is false or misleading.
- The package is missing the name & location of the manufacturer, packer, or distributor.
- The label or labeling is missing required information.
- A habit-forming drug is missing the name and amount of substance and the statement "Warning – May Be Habit Forming."
- It is a prescription drug and the established (generic) name of the drug is not printed on its label prominently and in type at least half as large as that used for the proprietary (brand) name.
- All drugs must have the drug's name on the label and prescription drugs must also have the quantity of the active ingredients (e.g. lisinopril 10mg). Any failure to meet this requirement will result in the drug being misbranded.
- It is missing adequate directions for use or adequate warnings. [OTC only]
- The drug is recognized in a compendium and is not packaged and labeled as required by the compendium's standards.
- The drug is dangerous when used in the dosage, or with the frequency or duration prescribed, recommended, or suggested in the labeling or advertising.
- If it is insulin or an applicable antibiotic (e.g. produced by

microorganisms - streptomycin), and does not have a required batch certificate of release in effect.
- If a trademark, trade name, or other identifying mark was placed on the drug or container with intent to defraud (counterfeit).
- If it is a prescription drug and its label does not contain its established name, the quantitative formula of each ingredient, and a necessary summary of information on side effects, contraindications, and effectiveness as specified by the Federal Food, Drug & Cosmetic Act's regulations.
- The labeling for prescription drug vials dispensed to patients by a pharmacy will be covered later in this text.

Prescriptions

According to guidelines published on the Virginia Board of Pharmacy web site, 30% of the exam will cover reviewing prescriptions. Pay special attention to the laws regulating prescription authority. It will also be important to understand the nuances of chart orders, orders for hospice patients, home infusion patients, and faxed and electronic prescriptions. As a pharmacist, you will be responsible for knowing if a prescription or order is valid or not.

Prescribing Authority

Does Virginia or the Federal government decide who has prescribing authority in Virginia?
Virginia does. State law controls who can write valid prescriptions.

What practitioners can write valid prescriptions for controlled substances in Virginia?
- Practitioners of medicine (Medical Doctor or M.D.)
- Practitioners of osteopathy (Osteopath or D.O.)

- Practitioners of dentistry (Dentist, D.D.S. or D.M.D.)
- Practitioners of podiatry (Podiatrist or D.P.M. – "foot doctor")
- Practitioners of veterinary medicine (Veterinarian or D.V.M.)
- Virginia licensed nurse practitioners (NP or FNP)
- Virginia licensed physician's assistants (PA)
- Virginia TPA-certified optometrists (O.D.)

Which prescribers have unrestricted prescribing authority and can write for CII-CVI prescriptions to treat their patients without the need for an agreement with any other practitioner?

- Medical doctors
- Osteopathic doctors
- Dentists
- Podiatrists
- Veterinarians

Can a Virginia pharmacy fill prescriptions written by out of state practitioners?

Yes, if the prescriber is a medical doctor, osteopath, dentist, podiatrist, or veterinarian and the prescription meets all of the other requirements for a valid Virginia issued prescription.

Out of state prescriptions from nurse practitioners, physicians' assistants, and optometrists are not valid unless the prescriber is licensed in Virginia in addition to the other state.

Are there any restrictions on the prescribing of drugs by medical doctors, osteopathic doctors, podiatrists, dentists, and veterinarians?

Yes. Medical doctors, osteopathic doctors, podiatrists, and dentists can not write prescriptions for animals.

Veterinarians can only write prescriptions for animals.

Dentists can only write prescriptions for the treatment of mouth conditions and diseases. A prescription for oral contraceptives would not be valid.

Podiatrists can only write prescriptions for the treatment of conditions and diseases of the foot and ankle. A prescription for an asthma medication would not be valid.

What are the prescribing restrictions on nurse practitioners and physician assistants?

A nurse practitioner's prescribing authority is dependent upon entry into a practice agreement with a patient care team physician that clearly states the prescriptive practices of the nurse practitioner.

A physician assistant's prescribing authority is dependent upon entry into a written agreement with a licensed physician or podiatrist that provides for the direction and supervision of the physician assistant's prescriptive practices.

How will you know if a nurse practitioner or physician's assistant is prescribing a drug that is not allowed under his agreement with a team care physician, physician or podiatrist?

You may not be able to tell if the prescription is for an approved drug. But, you should examine the practice the prescriber is in to make sure that the prescription is for a drug that would normally be prescribed in that practice setting. For example, if you received a prescription for oral contraceptives from a NP at an OB/GYN practice, the prescription is most probably within the NP's scope of practice. However, if that same NP wrote a prescription for treatment of gum disease (chlorhexidine), you would want to call the doctor's office to verify the prescription.

Are nurse practitioners and physician assistants allowed to write CII through CVI prescriptions?

Yes.

Are there any prescribing limitations on TPA-certified optometrists?

Yes.

What medications are TPA certified optometrists allowed to prescribe and administer?

- CIII-VI oral analgesics to relieve ocular (eye) pain
- Other oral CVI controlled substances to treat diseases of the eye and it's adnexa
- Topically applied CVI drugs (for treatment of the eye/adnexa)

- Intramuscular administration of epinephrine to treat emergency cases of anaphylactic shock

What is the "adnexa" of the eye?

The tissues immediately surrounding the eye; such as the eyelids and conjunctiva.

What certification does an optometrist (OD) need in order to prescribe?

TPA-certification. TPA stands for Therapeutic Pharmaceutical Agents.

Is TPA-certification a state or national certification?

It is a Virginia certification that ODs must obtain from the Virginia Board of Optometry.

What conditions are TPA certified optometrists allowed to treat?

Diseases and abnormal conditions of the human eye and its adnexa (tissues adjoining the eye).

Are there any conditions that TPA-certified optometrists are specifically prohibited from treating?

Yes. Optometrists cannot treat infantile or congenial glaucoma and their treatment of closed angle glaucoma is limited to initiation of immediate emergency care.

Are pharmacies allowed to supply TPA-certified optometrists with therapeutic pharmaceutical agents listed on the TPA-Formulary?

Yes.

Are medical interns and residents who work in a hospital allowed to write prescriptions?

Yes, but only within their duties as part of the residency program. This may include writing prescriptions for ER patients that will be filled at a retail pharmacy.

Prescriptions and Chart Orders

What is a "prescription" under Virginia law?

An order for drugs or medical supplies, given to a pharmacist by a practitioner authorized to prescribe. The prescription may be written, oral, faxed or transmitted electronically.

What prescriber information must every Virginia prescription contain?

- Prescriber's name
- Prescriber's address
- Prescriber's phone number
- Prescriber's signature (except for on oral prescriptions)
- Are there any additional requirements for Federally controlled substance prescriptions (CII-V)? 21 CFR 1306.05, 54.1-3408.01
- Yes. They must also contain the prescriber's DEA number.

Are medical interns and residents allowed to write prescriptions in Virginia?

Yes.

Since interns and some residents do not have a DEA number, what do they use in place of their own DEA number?

They use the hospital where they are practicing's DEA number plus a suffix assigned to the intern/resident by the institution. (E.g. BB1438901-1234)

Do intern and resident's prescriptions need to comply with all of the regular requirements for a valid Virginia prescription?

Yes.

Are the interns/residents allowed to use their identification number to write for CII-CVI controlled substances?

Yes.

When can a medical intern or resident working for a hospital prescribe controlled substances under the hospital's DEA number?

When it is in furtherance of the person's duties at the hospital. The intern or resident cannot use the number if he/she is working somewhere else like an urgent care center that is not affiliated with the hospital.

What if the patient was seen by the intern/resident at the hospital's emergency room?

The intern/resident can use the hospital identification number assigned to him to write a prescription for the patient.

What other information has to go on the prescription?

- The intern/resident's signature and the legibly printed name, address, and telephone number of the resident/intern.
- The address and phone number are usually pre-printed on the hospital's prescription blank but the intern/resident's information is often not included and must be added by hand.

Who else is exempt from the requirement to register with the DEA?

- Agents and employees of registrants (e.g., employees of a pharmacy)
- Practitioners affiliated with registrants (e.g., doctors working at a hospital)
- Law enforcement officials

What patient information must be on the prescription?

- The patient's first and last name
- The patient's address

What if the patient is an animal?

The prescription must contain the:

- Owner's name
- Owner's address
- The species of the animal

Does the prescriber need to write the patient's address on the prescription?

No, it can be added by the dispenser or kept in the patient's electronic record in the pharmacy.

Does the prescription need to be dated?

Yes. It must be dated on the date it is signed by the prescriber. Postdating of prescriptions is not allowed and is illegal.

What drug information must go on the prescription?
- Drug name
- Drug strength
- Drug dosage form
- Quantity prescribed
- Directions for use

Virginia doesn't specifically require a quantity on prescriptions for CVI drugs provided that the prescription contains some directions by which the pharmacist can calculate the authorized quantity using directions for use and duration. CII-CV prescriptions must contain a quantity.

How long are long are prescriptions for CII-CV drugs valid?
Six months from the date of issuance.

How long is a prescription for a CVI drug valid?
It is valid for one year after the date of issue, which means that you can continue to refill the prescription for up to one year after the date of issuance. However, if the prescriber specifically authorizes the dispensing or refilling of the prescription for two years, you can fill and refill the prescription for two years. This would apply if the prescriber wrote on the prescription: "May refill prn for 2 years." If such instructions are not present, the prescription is only valid for one year.

Can a prescription be written in pencil?
No. Prescriptions must be written in ink, individually typed, or printed only.

How many medications can be on a single prescription form?
The general rule is only one medication per prescription.

What are the exceptions to the general rule?
- Prescriptions written as chart orders for patients in hospitals
- Prescriptions written as chart orders for patients in long term care facilities
- Patients receiving home infusion services
- Hospice patients

- Patients whose prescriptions will be filled at pharmacies operated by one of these departments: Corrections, Juvenile Justice, Health, Behavioral Health and Development Services
- Patients residing in detention centers, jails, or work release centers operated by the Dept. of Corrections

All of the exceptions include the use of chart orders or governmental provision of services.

What about prescriptions written as chart orders for a hospital or long term care patient who is then discharged?

These can be filled at an outpatient pharmacy if:

- The pharmacist has all the information necessary for a valid outpatient prescription
- The pharmacist has written or verbal directions indicating that the chart orders are intended to serve as prescription orders
- The orders include some directions related to the quantity to be dispensed or duration of the order.

Can you accept a post dated CII prescription?

No. It must be signed and dated on the day it was written.

Can you accept a post dated CIII-VI prescription?

No, it must be signed and dated on the day it was written.

When can a prescriber use a completely preprinted prescription form?

Only for CVI prescriptions and they will still need to sign the prescription.

Can a pharmacist accept oral or telephone prescriptions for CIII-CVI drugs in Virginia?

Yes.

Who is allowed to call in an oral prescription?

The prescriber or his authorized agent.

Who may act as the prescriber's "authorized agent"?

- An employee under the prescriber's immediate and personal supervision
- An individual holding a valid license allowing administration or

dispensing of drugs who has been specifically directed by the prescriber (e.g. a nurse or a pharmacist)

If a pharmacist receives an oral prescription but does not have the medication, can she phone the prescription in to another pharmacy of the patient's choice?

Yes. The pharmacist is licensed to dispense drugs and was specifically directed by the prescriber to have the medication dispensed to the patient.

Can a nurse call in a prescription for the doctor?

Yes, for CIII-VI drugs.

When a pharmacist receives an oral prescription, is she required to place any additional information on the prescription?

Yes. The pharmacist must reduce the prescription to writing and include the first and last name of the person who called in the prescription as well as a notation that the prescription was an oral order. The pharmacist must write (not sign) the prescriber's name on the prescription as well.

Can a community pharmacist ever accept a telephone (oral) prescription for a CII drug in a community pharmacy?

Yes, but only in emergencies and the quantity dispensed must be limited to that necessary to cover the emergency time period. The pharmacist should make a reasonable effort to confirm that the prescription really came from the prescriber. For example, if the pharmacist did not know the prescriber, he should look up the prescriber in the phonebook and call that number to confirm that the prescription is authentic. Only the actual prescriber can call in an emergency CII prescription.

What must the pharmacist do with the emergency CII oral prescription?

The pharmacist must reduce it to writing so that it has all of required elements for a written prescription except for the prescriber's signature.

Does the prescriber of the emergency CII oral prescription have to do anything else?

Yes. The prescriber must provide the pharmacy with an original signed CII written prescription to cover the emergency dispensing.

Are there any special requirements for the original signed CII

prescription?

Yes. It must be dated and signed on the date of the emergency oral prescription and must include the words: "authorization for emergency dispensing" on the face of the prescription. It must meet all of the usual requirements for a CII prescription.

What is the pharmacist required to do with the hard copy emergency prescription when he receives it?

Attach it to the emergency oral prescription and file it.

How long does the prescriber have to get the pharmacy the written CII prescription?

The prescriber has 7 days to provide the pharmacy will the written CII prescription. The prescriber can meet the 7 day deadline by mailing the prescription within 7 days of calling in the prescription. So, it may actually take more than 7 days for the pharmacy to receive the hard copy of the prescription.

What must the pharmacist do if the prescription is not received within 7 days?

Contact the prescriber to find out if it was mailed within the 7 day time frame. The pharmacist should call earlier to make sure that the prescriber does not miss the deadline.

Does the pharmacist have to do anything if the prescription is not received or mailed within the 7 day limit?

Yes. The pharmacist has to notify the DEA that the prescription was never received.

What happens if the pharmacist doesn't notify the DEA?

The pharmacist's authority under law to dispense an emergency CII prescription is revoked and the pharmacist can be found guilty of illegally distributing a CII drug!

Are oral orders for CII drugs allowed in a hospital?

Yes. A hospital pharmacist or nurse can take an oral order for a CII drug. It has to be immediately reduced to writing and signed by the prescriber within 72 hours.

Can a prescriber write multiple CII prescriptions for the same drug

for a single patient on the same day and place instructions on the prescriptions as to when they may be filled?

Yes. Each prescription must still be issued for a legitimate medical purpose by a prescriber acting in the usual course of his professional practice (see intangible prescription requirements below).

What are the requirements for the issuance of multiple CII prescriptions at the same time?

Each prescription, other than the first one to be filled, must indicate the earliest date that it can be filled.

The maximum days supply for multiple issued prescriptions is 90 days.

The prescriptions must meet all other requirements for valid CII prescriptions.

Are veterinarians allowed to write CII prescriptions for animals?

Yes. The same rules apply as for human CII prescriptions.

Are pharmacists allowed to make any changes to a written CII prescription?

Yes. A pharmacist may make the following changes to a hard copy CII prescription:

- Add or correct the patient's name after verifying it
- Add the patient's address after verifying it
- Add the prescriber's DEA number
- After direct consultation and agreement of the prescriber, the pharmacist can add or change dosage form, drug strength, directions for use, drug quantity, and issue date

What two changes are prohibited for CII prescriptions?

The pharmacist is never allowed to change the drug prescribed, other than generic substitution, or add the prescriber's signature to the prescription.

Are there any special requirements for a prescription that is written for gamma-hydroxybutyric acid (rohypnol)?

Yes. The medical need for the drug must be written on the prescription.

Are computer generated prescriptions allowed in Virginia?

Yes. The prescription must still be hand signed by the prescriber.

Does an order on a chart need to contain all the same information as a written prescription?

Not if the following conditions are met:

- The information is contained in other readily retrievable records of the pharmacy
- The pharmacy's policy and procedure manual sets out where this information is maintained and how to retrieve it
- The chart orders meet the minimum requirements for chart orders consistent with state and federal law and the accepted standard of care

Faxed Prescriptions

Can prescriptions for CIII-CVI drugs be faxed to a pharmacy?

Yes.

Is a faxed prescription required to have all of the information required on a regular written prescription?

YES! This includes the prescriber's signature.

Can a prescriber give an oral prescription to his agent to be faxed?

Yes. The faxed prescription must contain the agent's full name and language that indicates the prescription is an oral prescription. If the prescription is oral, the prescriber's signature does not have to be on the prescription.

Are faxed prescriptions required to have any additional information on them?

Yes. They must have the following additional information:

- Date the prescription was faxed
- Printed name, address, phone number, and fax number of the prescriber
- If faxed from an institution, the name, address, phone, and fax number of the institution.

Do regular written prescriptions need to have a fax number on them.?
No.

Who decides where the prescription will be faxed?
The patient gets to choose the pharmacy where the prescription will be faxed.

Where can a faxed prescription originate?
- The prescriber's practice location
- A faxed order received by a long term care facility may be forwarded to a pharmacy for filling
- A faxed order received by a hospice (including home hospice) may be forwarded to a pharmacy for filling
- A written prescription can be faxed by an authorized agent of a long term care facility if the pharmacy has written procedures. The hard copy must be delivered to the pharmacy within 7 days and attached to the faxed copy.

When can a prescription for a CII drug be faxed?
For information purposes only. This does NOT count as the original written prescription but allows the pharmacy to prepare the prescription prior to receipt of the actual hard copy prescription. The original hard copy prescription must be received before the prescription can be dispensed to the patient. This would be done when a patient is being discharged from the hospital and should not be waiting at the pharmacy for any extended period of time.

Are there any times when a CII prescription can be faxed and actually filled?
Yes. Faxed CII prescriptions are valid for:
- Long term care facility patients,
- Home infusion patients, and
- Medicare certified hospice patients; including home hospice patients. [The prescriber must note on the prescription that the patient is in hospice.]

Electronic Prescriptions

Does Virginia allow allow the electronic transmission of prescriptions from prescribers to pharmacies?

Yes.

What is an electronic prescription?

A prescription that is generated using an electronic application and transmitted to a pharmacy as an electronic data file.

What schedules of drugs can be transmitted as electronic prescriptions?

Schedules II, III, IV, V, and VI.

How does a prescriber apply for authorization to issue electronic prescriptions for CII-CV drugs?

A prescriber applies to a federally approved credential service provider (CSP) or certification authority (CA) to obtain a two-factor authentication credential or a digital certificate.

Does an electronic prescription have to be manually signed?

No. It will contain an electronic or digital signature that identifies the prescriber as the source of the prescription and indicate his approval of the information contained in the prescription.

What Federal requirements do electronic prescriptions have to meet?

Security and authentication features

Required recordkeeping by the prescriber and the pharmacy

Are there any requirements for the provider of the electronic applications used by the prescribers and pharmacies for CII-CV electronic applications?

Yes. The provider must be reviewed and certified as compliant with the DEA's standards by an approved certification body, which will issue it a certification report.

How will a pharmacy or prescriber know that the application provider is certified?

The application provider must provide a copy of its certification report to the pharmacy or prescriber.

Can a pharmacy process an electronic prescription and dispense a CII-CV drug before the certification report is received?

NO. The pharmacy can process and dispense CVI prescriptions in compliance with the Board's regulations prior to receiving the report but cannot receive and dispense CII-CV prescriptions until the report is received.

Can an electronic prescription be converted to a fax and printed out on the pharmacy's fax machine?

Only if the prescription is for a CVI substance. CII-CV electronic prescriptions are prohibited by Federal law from being converted to a faxed prescription. CII-CV electronic prescriptions are required to directly populate the pharmacy's automated dispensing system in accordance with Federal law.

What are the requirements for transmission of electronic prescriptions?

- The prescriptions need to be transmitted by the prescriber or his authorized agent directly to the pharmacy.
- Electronic prescriptions for CII-CV medications must comply with the security and other requirements set forth in Federal law.
- Electronic prescriptions need to comply with Virginia's security requirements related to the protection of patient health information.

Who decides which pharmacy will receive an electronic prescription?

The patient. An electronic prescription must be transmitted to the patient's pharmacy of choice.

What information does an electronically transmitted prescription need to include?

- All of the information required for a written prescription
- The full name of the prescriber's agent if the prescriber is not transmitting the electronic prescription
- Date of transmission

What does a pharmacist have to do when she receives a paper or oral

prescription that was originally electronically transmitted to the pharmacy?

The pharmacist has to check the pharmacy's record to make sure that the electronic version was not received and dispensed. If the pharmacy received both prescriptions, the pharmacist will have to mark one of the prescriptions as void.

What does a pharmacist have to do when she receives a paper or oral prescription that was originally electronically transmitted to another pharmacy?

The pharmacist has to check with the other pharmacy to determine if the prescription was received and dispensed by the other pharmacy. If the other pharmacy received but did not already dispense the medication, that pharmacy must mark the electronic prescription as void or cancelled. If the other pharmacy already dispensed the prescription, the pharmacist must mark the paper copy as void and not dispense it.

Intangible Prescription Requirements

What is the difference between an "intangible" and a "tangible" prescription requirement?

You can see a tangible prescription requirement and cannot see an intangible prescription requirement. An example of a "tangible" requirement is the signature of the prescriber, which you can see is either on or not on the prescription. You cannot see whether a prescription was issued for a medicinal or therapeutic purpose. Instead, you have to use your judgment to determine whether the prescription was issued for a valid medicinal purpose.

Are there "intangible" prescription requirements in Virginia?

Yes. A prescription is not valid unless it was:

- Issued for a medicinal or therapeutic purpose
- To a patient with whom the practitioner has a bona fide practitioner-patient relationship.

What does the practitioner have to do to create a bona fide practitioner-patient relationship?

- Obtain a medical or drug history
- Provide information to the patient about the benefits and risks of the drug being prescribed
- Perform an appropriate examination of the patient, either physically or by using equipment to electronically transmit images and medical records
- Except for medical emergencies, the examination of the patient should be performed by the practitioner, within the group in which he or she practices, or by a consulting practitioner
- Initiate additional interventions and follow-up care, if necessary, especially if a prescribed drug may have serious side effects

When is a bona fide practitioner patient relationship deemed to exist by law or not needed for the issuance of a valid prescription?

The practitioner does not have to personally examine the partner of one of his patients with whom he has a bona fide practitioner patient relationship in order to issue the partner a prescription for a CVI antibiotic to treat a communicable disease (e.g. syphilis) in accordance with CDC guidance to prevent imminent risk of death, illness or serious disability.

Practice tip: there are other situations where protocols, such as for the administration of vaccines in hospitals, substitute for the bona fide relationship.

What are the potential consequences for a pharmacist who knowingly fills an invalid prescription?

The pharmacist may be criminally prosecuted for drug distribution!

What does Virginia law require a pharmacist to do when presented with a questionable prescription?

The pharmacist must contact the prescriber or his agent and verify:

- The patient's identity
- The name of the medication prescribed
- The quantity of the medication prescribed

If a pharmacist satisfies Virginia's requirements for handling a questionable prescription, are the Federal DEA requirements satisfied?

NO! Simply calling the doctor's office and verifying the information required under Virginia law will not satisfy the DEA. The DEA expects a pharmacist to be aware of prescribing habits, excessive quantities, multiple prescriptions, and other indicators of improper prescribing when such information is readily available or easily obtainable by the pharmacist. This would not apply to CVI prescriptions.

When does a bona fide practitioner-patient-pharmacist relationship exist?

When the practitioner prescribes, and a pharmacist dispenses, controlled substances in good faith to his patient for a medicinal or therapeutic purpose within the course of his professional practice.

What are some examples of a prescriber issuing prescriptions that are not within her course of professional practice?

- A podiatrist (DPM) issuing a prescription for treatment of a sinus infection. (Podiatrists are only allowed to treat conditions of the feet/ankle)
- A dentist (D.D.S. or D.M.D.) issuing a prescription for birth control.
- A doctor (M.D.) issuing a prescription to treat an animal.
- A veterinarian (D.V.M.) issuing a prescription to treat a human.
- An optometrist (O.D.) issuing a prescription to treat a sore throat.

Practice tip: medical doctors and osteopaths are allowed to write prescriptions to treat almost any human condition. And, the specialty of the medical doctor or osteopath does not change this. For example: a psychiatrist can prescribe birth control pills and a surgeon can prescribe eye drops.

What must a pharmacist do if he declines to fill a prescription for any reason other than the unavailability of the drug?

Write the following on the back of the prescription:

- The word "Declined"
- The name, address, and telephone number of the pharmacy
- The date the prescription was declined
- The pharmacist's signature

What is a pharmacist required to do if he determines that a prescription is a forgery?

- Refrain from returning the prescription to the patient
- Maintain the prescription for a minimum of 30 days prior to destroying it
- Provide the prescription to a law enforcement official who is investigating the forgery

Dispensing and Distribution

According to guidelines published on the Virginia Board of Pharmacy's web site, 25% of the exam will cover dispensing and distribution. Be sure you understand which tasks may be performed by a technician or intern, and which are restricted to pharmacists. It is also important to understand refills and partial fills. As the pharmacist, you will have ultimate responsibility for ensuring that refills and partial fills are handled in accordance with the law.

Refills and Partial Fills

How long is a CII prescription valid in Virginia and how many times can it be refilled?

CII prescriptions are valid for 6 months and cannot be refilled.

How long are CIII - CV prescriptions valid in Virginia and how many times can they be refilled?

CIII-CV prescriptions are valid for 6 months and may be refilled a maximum of 5 times.

How long are CVI prescriptions valid in Virginia and how many times can they be refilled?

CVI prescriptions with no additional notations are valid for one year. As previously covered, the prescriber can specifically extend the time that a CVI prescription may be filled up to two years. There are no specific limits on the number of refills that a prescriber can include on a CVI prescription and a pharmacist can continue to refill the CVI prescription until it expires.

What can a pharmacist do if the patient needs a refill for a CVI drug and the prescriber is not available?

Virginia allows a CVI medication prescription to be refilled by a pharmacist without authorization from the prescriber if:

- The pharmacist has a made reasonable effort to contact the prescriber and
- The patient's health would be in imminent danger without the drug.

Are there any other requirements?

Yes. The pharmacist has to:

- Inform the patient that the refill is being made without the prescriber's authorization
- Inform the prescriber of the refill
- Document on the back of the prescription the date and quantity of the refill, the prescriber's unavailability, and the reason for the refill

Are pharmacists allowed to refill CIII-CVI prescriptions any time the patient requests a refill? 18 VAC110-20-320

No. Authorized refills may only be dispensed in reasonable conformity with the prescriber's directions for use. If there are no directions for use, the authorized refills may only be dispensed in reasonable conformity with the recommended dosages for the particular medication. This requires the pharmacist to exercise sound professional judgment. A pharmacist can refill a prescription early provided he documents a valid reason for the early refill. This documentation should be either on the actual prescription or in the electronic recordkeeping system of the pharmacy.

Does Virginia allow you to partially fill a CIII, CIV or CV prescription?

Yes. You can partially fill CIII-CV prescriptions provided that:

- The total quantity dispensed does not exceed the total quantity prescribe
- All partial dispensings take place during the six months that the prescription is valid
- The partial dispensings are done in reasonable conformity with the

directions for use of the medication or within the pharmacist's sound professional judgment
- Each partial dispensing is recorded in the same manner as a refill (covered later)

Partial dispensing example:

A patient receives a prescription for clonazepam 0.5 mg daily, #30, with 5 refills. The pharmacist can partially dispense 15 tablets to the patient every two weeks until the entire amount of the prescription, 180 tablets, has been dispensed. All partial dispensings have to take place before the 6 month expiration of the prescription.

Do partial dispensings appear to violate the 5 refill limit rule?

Yes. But, it is the law.

Can a prescriber fax a refill authorization for a CIII-CVI medication?

Yes.

What information does a faxed refill authorization need to include?

- Date of authorization
- Patient's name and address
- Drug name, strength and quantity
- Directions for use
- Prescriber's name
- Prescriber's signature or agent's first and last name for an oral prescription

Are pharmacists allow to partially dispense CVI medications as well?

Yes. A CVI prescription can be partially dispensed until the prescription expires or the quantity prescribed is reached. (e.g. Synthroid 50 mcg, 90 tabs, with 3 refills equals a maximum dispensed quantity of 90 X 4 = 360 tablets).

Are community pharmacists allowed to partially fill a prescription for a CII drug?

Yes, If the pharmacy does not have enough medication to completely fill the prescription.

Are there specific requirements concerning when the pharmacy can fill the remainder of the prescription?

Yes. The remainder of the prescription must be dispensed within 72 hours of the partial dispensing.

What happens if the pharmacist is unable to supply the remainder of the prescription within the 72 hour time frame?

The pharmacist cannot dispense the remainder of the CII prescription and must notify the prescriber that the patient only received the quantity of the partial dispensing. The patient will need a new prescription to receive any additional medication.

Are there any additional documentation requirements that apply when a pharmacist partially fills a CII prescription for lack of drug?

Yes. The pharmacist must record on the face of the prescription the amount partially dispensed and the date.

Are there other situations when a pharmacy may partially dispense CII prescriptions?

Yes. Pharmacies are allowed to partially dispense CII prescriptions for patients who are documented as being terminally ill and for patients in long term care facilities.

What does it mean for a patient to be "terminally ill"?

The patient must have a condition from which, to a reasonable degree of medical probability, he is unlikely to recover and be either:

- Close to death or
- In a persistent vegetative state

How does a patient get documented as being terminally ill?

The practitioner must classify the patient as terminally ill and the pharmacist must verify and record the patient's status on the prescription.

How long can a terminally ill or long term care patient continue to receive partial fills of a CII drug?

60 days from the date of the first partial filling unless the prescription expires earlier (6 months from date of issuance) or is discontinued by the prescriber. As always, the total quantity dispensed cannot exceed the

amount prescribed. The pharmacist must continually determine that the partial fills are necessary.

Are there any special recordkeeping requirements that apply when a pharmacist is partially dispensing a CII medication for a terminally ill or long term care patient?

Yes. Every time the pharmacist does a partial dispensing he has to record the following on the back of the prescription:

- The date of dispensing
- The quantity dispensed
- The remaining quantity authorized to be dispensed, and
- The pharmacist's identity

Can a pharmacy maintain computerized records of the partial dispensings of CII prescriptions for terminally ill patients and patients in a long-term care facility?

Yes, if the system allows immediate (real-time) updates every time a partial dispensing occurs and can produce an output showing:

- The original prescription number
- The prescription's date of issuance
- The identification of the prescriber
- The identification of the patient
- The identification of the long-term care facility (not a terminally ill patient)
- The identification of drug, including dosage form, strength, and quantity
- The listing of each partial dispensing under the prescription, and
- The information that would go on the back of the prescription if the pharmacy were manually maintaining the records.

Pharmacy Practice & Dispensing

What is the definition of "dispense" under Virginia law?

To deliver a drug to an ultimate user, research facility, or practitioner pursuant to a lawful order of a practitioner. If a doctor gives medications to patients to take with them from the office, his actions meet the definition of dispensing under Virginia law. Transporting drugs from the doctor's Arlington office to the Falls Church office is not dispensing.

What dispensing activities are restricted to pharmacists?

- The review of prescriptions for all legal and clinical requirements
- The receipt of a new oral prescription (technicians can take refills with no changes)
- The conducting of a prospective drug review
- The counseling of patients and the provision of drug information
- The communication with prescribers or agents regarding changes to therapy (other than refills where there are no changes to the prescription)
- The verification of the accuracy of a prescription prior to dispensing
- The supervision of pharmacy interns and technicians

Are pharmacy interns allowed to do activities that are restricted to pharmacists?

Yes, as long as the intern is being directly monitored by the pharmacist.

Can a non-pharmacist owner of a pharmacy make decisions that override the clinical decisions of the PIC or the pharmacist on duty?

No. That would be considered practicing pharmacy without a license.

When is a pharmacist required to conduct a prospective drug review?

Before each new prescription is dispensed or delivered. [Mandatory!]

Before refilling a prescription, if needed based on the pharmacist's professional clinical judgment.

What issues are screened for during a prospective drug review?

- Therapeutic duplication
- Drug-disease contraindications
- Drug-drug interactions, including nonprescription drugs
- Incorrect drug dosage

- Incorrect duration of drug treatment
- Drug-allergy interactions
- Clinical abuse or misuse

Are hospital pharmacists required to review drug therapy for hospital patients? 54.1-3319

Yes. Each order should be subjected to the same type of prospective drug review noted in the previous question. Ensuring that this occurs is the responsibility of the PIC.

Are there any special requirements for reviewing the drug therapy of patients in long-term care facilities?

Yes. A pharmacist must conduct a monthly review of the drug therapy of patients in long-term care facilities to check for irregularities, such as: drug therapy, drug interactions, and drug administration or transcription errors.

Does a pharmacist have to make an offer to counsel a patient prior to the dispensing of a new prescription?

Yes. For refills, the offer to counsel only needs to be made when the pharmacist deems it necessary based on her clinical judgment.

How may the offer to counsel be extended to the patient?

- Face-to-face
- Via a sign
- Via a notation on the bag
- Via telephone

Does a pharmacy need to make "reasonable efforts" to collect patient health information in order to provide pharmacy services?

YES.

What patient health information should the pharmacy make reasonable efforts to collect?

- The patient's name, address, date of birth, gender, and phone number
- The patient's medical history, including any allergies and drug reactions
- A list of the patient's current medications and devices

- Whether the patient accepted or failed to accept the pharmacist's offer to counsel

What is the implication of a pharmacy's failure to document a patient's refusal to accept counselling?

The law will presume that the offer was accepted and that counseling was provided.

Is a pharmacist required to counsel patients in a hospital or nursing home?

No.

After an order has been prepared, what is a pharmacist required to do before the order can be delivered to the patient?

The pharmacist must inspect the order, verify its accuracy in all respects, and initial the dispensing record to certify the accuracy of the prescription.

Does a pharmacist, or his agent, have to require proof of identity at the time of delivery before dispensing a CII drug to a person if the person is not known to the pharmacist or his agent?

Yes.

What if the person picking up the CII prescription is not the patient?

The pharmacy has to make a photocopy or electronic copy of the person's ID or record the full name and address of the person.

How long does the pharmacy have to keep the identification records?

At least one month.

Is a pharmacist permitted to require proof of identify from any patient presenting a CIII-CV prescription or requesting a refill of a CIII-CV prescription?

Yes. A pharmacist has the discretion to require proof of identity for CIII-CV prescriptions but is not mandated to do so.

What are acceptable forms of proof of identification?

- A driver's license
- A government-issued identification card, or
- Other photo identification along with documentation of the person's

current address.

What is required when a pharmacist delivers a CII drug by mail, common carrier or delivery service to a Virginia address?

The delivery method must require the signature of the recipient as confirmation of receipt.

Prescription Transfers

Does Virginia allow pharmacies to transfer prescriptions to other pharmacies?

Yes. The patient must consent and the prescription must be eligible for filling or refilling.

Are CII prescriptions that have not been filled transferrable?

CII prescriptions cannot be transferred.

What methods may be used to transfer a prescription?

- Orally by direct communication between two pharmacists
- By fax machine
- By electronic transmission

What is the transferring pharmacy required to do?

Write "VOID" on the face of the invalidated prescription.

Record the following information on the back of the prescription:

- Date of the transfer
- Name of the receiving pharmacy
- Address of the receiving pharmacy
- The DEA number of the receiving pharmacy for CIII-CV drugs
- For oral transfers, the first and last name of the pharmacist receiving the prescription

What is the receiving pharmacy required to do?

- Write the word "TRANSFER" on the face of the transferred

prescription
- Obtain and record all required information for a regular prescription

What additional information is the receiving pharmacy required to record on the transferred prescription?

- The date of issuance of the original prescription
- The original number of refills authorized on the original prescription
- The date of original dispensing, if applicable
- The number of valid refills remaining and the date of the last dispensing
- The transferring pharmacy's name, address, DEA registry number (unless a CVI drug)
- The original prescription number from the transferring pharmacy
- The first and last name of the transferring pharmacist, if transferred orally

How long do the pharmacies need to keep the transferred prescription records?

Both the original and transferred prescription must be maintained for two years from the date of last refill.

Can you give a patient a copy of a prescription after it has been transferred?

You may give the patient a copy of the prescription marked "For Information Only." You can do this for any prescription in your pharmacy.

Instead of writing the information on the transferred prescription, can the transferring pharmacy record this information electronically in an automated data processing system?

Yes, as long as the system meets the requirements for storage and retrieval of dispensing information for automated dispensing systems.

If a patient transfers a prescription between pharmacies that share a common database (most chain pharmacies), does the receiving pharmacy have to print and maintain a hard copy of the prescription?

Not if the pharmacies share a common database that is capable of generating a hard copy of the transferred prescription upon request.

How many times can a prescription for a CVI drug be transferred?

Until the prescription runs out of refills.

How many times can a prescription for a CII drug be transferred?

NONE! Trick question.

How many times can a prescription for a CIII, CIV, or CV drug be transferred?

One time only; unless the pharmacies share a common database.

How many times can a prescription for a CIII, CIV, or CV drug be transferred between pharmacies that share an electronic real-time online database?

Until the prescription is out of refills or expires.

Are there any additional record keeping requirements for transfers of

Yes. You are required to record the date(s) and locations of previous refills. [State law only requires you to record the date of original and last dispensing and does not require you to record the location of each refill]

Generic Substitution

How does Virginia refer to drugs approved for generic substitution?

Therapeutically equivalent drug products.

What is a therapeutically equivalent drug product?

A drug product that has the same active ingredient(s), strength or concentration, dosage form, and route of administration as the brand name product. It must also be classified as being therapeutically equivalent in the FDA's most recent edition of the Approved Drug Products with Therapeutic Equivalence Evaluations, otherwise known as the "Orange Book."

When is a pharmacist prohibited from substituting a generic drug for the brand name drug when filling a prescription?

- When a therapeutically equivalent drug product is not available
- When the prescriber writes "brand medically necessary" on the

prescription
- When the prescriber requested the brand name drug on an oral prescription
- When the patient requests the brand name drug

Can a pharmacist substitute a generic drug and charge the patient more than the patient would have been charged for the brand name product?
NO!

What is a pharmacist required to do when she dispenses a generic drug in place of the brand name drug prescribed?
- Inform the patient
- Indicate on the patient record and the prescription label the therapeutically equivalent drug product and the name of the drug's manufacturer or distributor
- Label the prescription vial with the drug product dispensed followed by "generic for" and the brand name. (see labeling section)
- Charge the patient less than the cost of the brand name product prescribed

Prescription Labeling

What pharmacy information needs to be on label of a prescription vial dispensed to a patient?
- The pharmacy or pharmacist's name
- The pharmacy's address

Does the prescriber's name need to appear on prescription label?
Yes.

What other information needs to appear on the prescription label?
- The prescription number
- The date of the prescription or of its filling

- The patient's name
- The owner's name and species of the animal if for an animal
- The drug name
- The drug strength, if applicable
- The directions for use; including cautionary statements if included on the prescription
- The quantity dispensed; in dosage units or milliliters for a liquid
- For any single ingredient brand name drug dispensed, the drug's generic name in addition to the brand name
- If the prescription was written for a brand name drug and a generic drug is being dispensed, the words "generic for" followed by the brand name, and the generic drug's manufacturer or distributor
- For CII-IV drugs, "Caution: Federal law prohibits the transfer of this drug to any person other than the patient for whom it was prescribed."

Are medications dispensed for patients in hospitals and long term care facilities required to meet these same labeling requirements?

Not if the drugs are being administered by persons who are licensed to administer medications.

What is the definition of "administer" under Virginia law?

The direct application of a controlled substance to the body of a patient or research subject by a practitioner or her agent, or by the patient under the direction of the practitioner.

What is an example of drug repackaging?

Compounding batch dose IVs for future use. For example, a hospital pharmacy may compound diltiazem, vancomycin, and phenylephrine IVs for future use.

When a pharmacist repackages a drug, what information must go on the label?

- Drug name
- Drug strength
- Lot or control number. This can be one assigned by the pharmacy or

you can list the manufacturers or distributors name and it's lot or control number.
- Appropriate expiration date determined by the pharmacist in accordance with USP guidelines.

Prescription Drug Packaging

What is a repackaged drug?

A drug that has been removed from the manufacturer's original package and placed in different packaging.

What types of packaging are pharmacists allowed to use to dispense prescriptions?

- USP-NF approved packaging
- Well-closed containers
- Compliance packaging when requested by the patient, or for use in hospitals or long-term care facilities

What is a "well closed container?"

A container that protects the contents from extraneous solids and drug loss during normal shipping and storage.

What is "compliance packaging?"

Packaging for solid oral dosage forms that consists of a series of containers designed to assist the user with correct administration or self-administration in accordance with the directions for use (e.g. a "pill minder").

What is a " safety closure container?"

A container that meets the requirements of the Federal Poison Prevention Packaging Act of 1970, which are as follows:

- Out of a group of 200 children age 41-52 months, 85% cannot open the package in 5 minutes
- After a demonstration of how to open the package, and 5 more minutes, 80% of the children still cannot open it, and
- 90% of adults can open and close it

What is "special packaging?"

Packaging that is designed to be difficult for children under 5 years of age to open. This is Virginia's version of a safety closure container.

Are pharmacists usually required to dispense prescriptions in special packaging?

Yes.

Is a patient allowed to request non-special packaging?

Yes. The patient can even make a valid request for all of his prescriptions to be dispensed in non-special packaging.

Can a prescriber request that a patient's medicine be dispensed in non-special packaging?

Yes, but the request is only valid per prescription. The pharmacy cannot honor a prescriber's request to dispense all of a patient's prescriptions in non-special packaging.

Does a pharmacy need to document a patient's request for non-special packaging?

Yes. A notation must be made on the dispensing record or other retrievable record and maintained for at least two years.

How can a pharmacist avoid civil liability when dispensing prescriptions in non-special packaging?

The pharmacist must have the patient sign a release covering a period of time or a single delivery, that releases the pharmacist from civil liability for not using a safety closure container. This will not protect a pharmacist who acted with willful and wanton disregard for safety.

Are there exceptions to the special packaging requirements?

Yes. Certain prescription drugs such as sublingual nitroglycerin, medrol dose packs and non-oral dosage forms are not required to be in special packaging.

Where can a pharmacist find more in-depth information regarding the Poison Prevention Packaging Act's requirements?

The U.S. Consumer Product Safety Commission's website: http://www.cpsc.gov/PageFiles/114277/384.pdf

Pharmacy Access

Can a pharmacy operate without having a pharmacist on duty?

No. The prescription department must be locked and alarmed when a pharmacist is not on duty.

Who is allowed to have the keys and alarm code to the pharmacy?

Only pharmacists who practice at the pharmacy and who are authorized by the PIC may have the keys and alarm code to the pharmacy.

Is a pharmacy allowed to store its CII drugs with the other schedules of drugs?

Yes, if they are dispersed throughout the pharmacy. Or, the CII drugs can be stored separately provided they are locked in a drawer, cabinet or safe.

If the CII drugs are stored in a locked safe, can the safe remain unlocked when there is a pharmacist on duty and the prescription department is open?

Yes.

Where are expired medications stored?

They must be kept in the prescription department separated from the other drugs.

Is the PIC allowed to keep a key available for emergencies?

Yes, the key and alarm access code may be placed in a sealed envelope or other container with the pharmacist's signature across the seal. It must be kept in a safe or vault within the pharmacy or other secured place for use by another pharmacist to gain access to the pharmacy.

If the pharmacist is unavailable, can a technician go into the prescription department to get a prescription that has already been filled and checked?

Yes, but only in an emergency. An emergency includes an unplanned absence of a pharmacist scheduled to work during regular pharmacy hours and an inability to obtain alternate pharmacist coverage. The technician must be accompanied by a member of the pharmacy's management or administration.

Does the technician need permission to enter the prescription department in the absence of a pharmacist?

Yes, the verbal permission (via phone) of the PIC or another pharmacist regularly employed by the pharmacy is required.

What are the recordkeeping requirements when a technician enters the pharmacy in an emergency situation without a pharmacist present?

A record must be made that includes:

- Date and time of entry
- The name and signature of the pharmacy technician
- The name, title, and signature of the person accompanying the pharmacy technician
- The pharmacist's name who granted the technician permission to enter the pharmacy
- The telephone number where that pharmacist was reached
- The name of the patient initially requesting the needed medication
- The nature of the emergency
- A listing of all prescriptions retrieved during that entry
- The time of the technician exited and re-secured the prescription department.

How long does the technician entry record need to be maintained?

For one year.

What happens to the key after the technician exits the pharmacy?

The technician is required to reseal the key and alarm code and place it back in the safe or vault.

Will the alarm code need to be changed?

Yes. The PIC must change the alarm access code within 48 hours of the technician's entry.

Can prescriptions that have already been prepared and certified by a pharmacist be stored outside of the prescription department for

delivery to patients when a pharmacist is not on duty?

Yes, they may be placed in a secure area outside the prescription department provided that access to the prescriptions is restricted to designated clerical assistants.

If a prescription is delivered to a patient when a pharmacist is not present, are there any additional record keeping requirements?

Yes. A record must be kept that includes:

- The patient's name
- The prescription number(s)
- The date of delivery
- The signature of the person receiving the prescription

How long does this delivery record need to be maintained?

One year.

Are there any restrictions on who a pharmacy can employ and provide with access to Federal controlled substances?

Yes. The pharmacy cannot employ and provide access to Federal controlled substances to:

- Any person convicted of a felony offense relating to controlled substances
- Any person who had a DEA registration application denied or registration revoked or surrendered for cause.

Dispensing of Non-Prescription CV Controlled Substances

Are there CV controlled substances that can be dispensed without a prescription?

Yes, in small quantities. The drugs that can be sold are: opium, codeine, dihydrocodeinone, ethylmorphine, and diphenoxylate. The most commonly dispensed product in this category is Robitussin with codeine or its generic.

How can a pharmacist tell when a CV controlled substance may be

dispensed without a prescription?

The product will not be a prescription only product and will not have the "Rx Only" symbol on it.

What are the dispensing limits on each CV OTC substance per 48 hour period?

- 200 milligrams of opium
- 270 milligrams of codeine
- 130 milligrams of dihydrocodeinone
- 65 milligrams of ethylmorphine
- 32.5 mg of of diphenoxylate

Is a pharmacist allowed to remove the OTC CV drug from a stock bottle of prescription only medication and dispense the limited quantity in a regular prescription bottle?

NO. The labeling of the OTC CV product will have adequate directions for use and warnings against misuse that an RX product would not be required to have. These directions and warnings are much more detailed than what is placed on a prescription label.

** Be careful not to remove any of an OTC CV product's labeling or it will be misbranded! **

What are the requirements for selling a CV OTC substance without a prescription?

- It must be dispensed by a pharmacist.
- It must be dispensed directly to the person requesting it.
- The customer must provide proof of age (18 years or older).
- The pharmacist must use professional discretion to ensure that the preparation is being dispensed for medicinal use only.

When the pharmacy dispenses a CV OTC preparation without a prescription, what information must be recorded?

- The date of sale
- The name and quantity of the preparation

- The name and address of the person to whom the preparation is dispensed
- The initials of the dispensing pharmacist

How long does the pharmacy have to maintain the OTC CV record?
Two years from the date of sale.

Dispensing of Non-Prescription Insulin

Are some insulins available in Virginia without a prescription?
Yes. Many regular, NPH, and 70/30 insulins are available without a prescription.

How will a pharmacist know that a particular insulin does not require a prescription?
It will not have the "Rx Only" symbol on its labeling.

Who is allowed to sell insulin?
Insulin may only be sold by a licensed pharmacist or under the supervision of a licensed pharmacist.

Are there any special recordkeeping requirements when insulin is sold without a prescription?
No.

Dispensing of Non-Prescription Controlled Paraphernalia

Does Virginia restrict the sale of certain controlled paraphernalia?
Yes.

What controlled paraphernalia may only be sold by a pharmacist?
- Hypodermic needles & syringes
- Gelatin capsules
- Quinine or any of its salts in excess of ¼ ounce

What information is a person purchasing controlled paraphernalia required to produce?

- Identification, including proof of age when appropriate.
- A written, legitimate purpose for which the controlled paraphernalia is being purchased. This is not required for a "customer of known good standing."

When the pharmacy sells controlled paraphernalia, what information must be recorded?

- Date of dispensing
- The name and quantity of the device, item or substance
- The price at which it was sold
- The name and address of the person to whom the device, item or substance was dispensed
- The reason for its purchase
- The pharmacist's initials

Are there any age restrictions that apply to the purchase of controlled paraphernalia?

Controlled paraphernalia cannot be sold to someone under the age of 16 except by a physician or with a prescription.

Is the pharmacy responsible for safeguarding controlled paraphernalia?

Yes, the pharmacy must "exercise reasonable care in the storage, usage and disposition of such devices" to prevent diversion. Controlled paraphernalia and medical devices must be stored in or adjacent to the prescription department where the pharmacist can exercise "reasonable supervision and control."

If a pharmacist violates the laws that control the storage, distribution or recordkeeping of controlled paraphernalia, what are the possible legal consequences?

The pharmacist may be found guilty of a Class 1 misdemeanor.

Dispensing of Non-Prescription Methamphetamine Precursors

What methamphetamine precursors are regulated in Virginia?

Ephedrine and pseudoephedrine base along with their salts, isomers, or salts of isomers. These are referred to as scheduled listed chemical products ("SLCPs") in Federal law.

What are the quantity limits on the sale of SLCPs in Virginia?

3.6 grams per day

9 grams per 30 day period

The Federal mail order limit is 7.5 grams per 30 day period.

Where can a pharmacy display its SLCPs?

Behind the store counter where it cannot be accessed by consumers or locked in a case that requires store employee assistance for access.

Does a prospective purchaser of SLCPs have to present a photo identification?

Yes and the identification must have been issued by a governmental or educational institution.

What are the recordkeeping requirements for the sale of SLCPs?

The pharmacy has to maintain a written log or electronic system that contains the following information:

- Purchaser's name and address
- Purchaser's birth date
- Purchaser's signature
- The product name and quantity sold; and
- The date and time of the transaction.

Are there any reporting requirements related to the sale of SLCPs?

Yes, unless the pharmacy has obtained an exemption it must use an electronic recordkeeping and monitoring system to report all nonprescription sales of SLCPs.

If the electronic system generates a stop alert to the pharmacy, can the pharmacy still complete the sale of the SLCP?

Not unless the seller has a reasonable fear of imminent bodily harm if the sale is not completed.

Are SLCP purchasers required to sign the the record acknowledging an understanding of the applicable sales limit?

Yes. The acknowledgement also has to include that the provision of a false statement or misrepresentation can subject the purchaser to penalties under Title 18 of the United State Code.

How long is the pharmacy required to maintain SLCP sales transaction records?

For at least two years from the date of last entry.

Does the pharmacy have to provide police officers involved in the investigation of methamphetamine manufacturing with access to the SLCP records?

Yes.

Do the SLCP provisions apply to prescriptions for medications that contain an SLCP?

No. The provisions only apply to OTC sales of SLCPs.

What is the penalty under Virginia law for any person who willfully violates the SLCP provisions?

The person can be found guilty of a Class 1 misdemeanor.

Does Virginia law have a minimum age requirement to purchase SLCPs?

No. Federal law prohibits the purchase of SLCPs by minors under the age of 16.

Dispensing of Non-Prescription Dextromethorphan

Is a pharmacy allowed sell OTC dextromethorphan to anyone under the age of 18?

No.

If a pharmacist cannot reasonably presume from a purchaser's appearance that the purchaser is at least 25 years of age, are there any identification requirements the pharmacist must comply with before selling dextromethorphan to a patient?

Yes. The purchaser must produce a federal, state, or local government issued identification document that contains the purchaser's date of birth and picture.

Do the dextromethorphan restrictions apply if the drug is being dispensed pursuant to a prescription?

No.

Prescription Delivery

A pharmacy wants to offer prescription delivery services. Can the dispensed prescriptions be delivered to the patient's office or the patient's home?

Yes, prescriptions may be:

- Directly hand delivered to patient or to the patient's agent
- Delivered to the residence of the patient
- Delivered to a place holding a current permit, license, or registration with the Board that authorizes the possession of controlled substances
- Delivered to an alternate location only if allowed by Federal law and the Virginia Board of Pharmacy

Does it make a difference is the prescription is for a Federal controlled substance?

Yes. The general rule is that CII-CV prescriptions should only be hand delivered to:

- The patient
- His agent
- The patient's residence.

Can the pharmacy deliver a CVI dispensed prescription to another pharmacy?

Yes.

Can the pharmacy deliver a CVI dispensed prescription to the patient's doctor?

Only if the doctor is licensed to practice pharmacy or to sell controlled substances.

Can the pharmacy deliver a CVI dispensed prescription to a person or entity that has a controlled substances registration?

Only if the person or entity is authorized to sell the drug.

What sort of written notice must be included when a dispensed prescription is delivered, instead of being picked up at the pharmacy?

A notice alerting the consumer that chemical degradation of drugs may occur under certain circumstances, and providing a toll-free or local number the consumer can call with questions.

Ordering, Receiving, and Managing Drug Inventory

According to guidelines published on the Virginia Board of Pharmacy's web site 20% of the exam will cover ordering, receiving, and managing drug inventory. Especially for controlled substances, there are substantial inventory and recordkeeping requirements. It is crucial that you understand these laws and regulations. In the eyes of the law, ignorance is no excuse. As a licensed pharmacist, you are expected to know the law and comply with it.

Pay particular attention to use of DEA form 222 and Schedule II drug transfers. Sections with relatively new material, such as compounding and the Prescription Monitoring Program are also worthy of attention.

Drug Acquisition

Who is allowed to purchase Schedule VI drugs and devices from a manufacturer or wholesaler?

Anybody who is authorized to administer, prescribe, or dispense the drug/device.

Who is allowed to purchase CII-VI drugs from a manufacturer or wholesaler?

- Another permitted manufacturer or wholesaler*
- A licensed pharmacist, permitted pharmacy, or licensed practitioner of medicine, osteopathy, podiatry, dentistry, or veterinary medicine*
- A person or entity that has been issued a Virginia Controlled Substances Registration Certificate if authorized by the certificate (the certificate specifies what schedules the holder is allowed to have)*
- A Federal, state, territorial, district, county, municipal, or insular government official when necessary for that person's official duties; a special written order and certificate of exemption is required.
- A ship or aircraft captain ("Master"), if there is no regular doctor on board, for the actual medical needs of persons on board. The vessel cannot be in port. This transfer requires approval of a special order from by a U.S. Public Health Service official or commissioned medical officer.
- A person in a foreign country in compliance with relevant federal laws.

*These persons and entities are also required to have a DEA registration to receive CII-CV drugs.

Are there any special requirements when the transfer involves a CII drug?

Yes, a DEA Form 222 (written or electronic) is required for all transfers of CII drugs. The only times a DEA Form 222 is not required is when a CII drug is being dispensed or administered to a patient, which requires a prescription or order, or when the CII drug is going from a central fill pharmacy to a retail pharmacy.

For the remainder of this text, "DEA Form 222" may be abbreviated "DEA 222 form" or "DEA 222."

From what entities are pharmacies allowed to purchase their CII-CVI medications?

Wholesale distributors and warehousers that have a license or registration from the Board.

What about in the case of an emergency?

In an emergency, a pharmacy may purchase CII-CVI drugs from another pharmacy. Remember, the transfer of a CII drug will require the use of a DEA 222.

Can drugs be transferred between a health care entities' hospitals?

Yes, if they are under common control. Remember, the transfer of a CII drug will require the use of a DEA 222.

Prescription Drug Returns

Is a pharmacy allowed to accepted, for re-dispensing, a prescription that was already dispensed to a patient? 54.1-3411.1

Only when the medication is in the manufacturer's original sealed container and USP storage requirements are assured.

For example: the dispensed prescription was for #20 Augmentin tablets and the pharmacy dispensed the unopened original stock bottle of 20 tablets to the patient. The patient was a pharmacist or physician who can reasonably be relied upon to inform the dispensing pharmacy of the conditions under which the prescription was held. This is a very rare circumstance as the pharmacist should not rely upon a layperson's word as to how the drug was stored.

A patient brings in an unused, unopened bottle of tablets that she picked up earlier today. The patient's doctor started her on a different drug this afternoon. The drug is in the manufacturer's original container, and the seal over the top is intact. Can the pharmacist re-dispense the drug to somebody else?

No. It's been out of possession of pharmacy personnel and the pharmacist cannot be assured that it was stored in compliance with USP standards.

What if the patient paid for the prescription and immediately realized she had called in the wrong refill?

If it hasn't left the pharmacy premises, the medication can be accepted for return and re-dispensing.

Can the pharmacy take a prescription that was awaiting delivery to the patient in the will call bin and return it to the shelf for re-dispensing?

Yes.

How is the pharmacy required to handle the storage and dispensing of the drug that was returned from the will call bin?

An expiration date must be placed on the prescription label prior to returning the drug to stock.

If the pharmacy does not have stability data to the contrary, the expiration date added to the label cannot exceed the earlier of one year from the date the prescription was filled or the expiration date on the stock bottle.

The restocked drug must be used to fill the next prescription received for that product. If the drug is not dispensed prior to the newly assigned expiration date, the drug must be removed from stock and disposed of in accordance with the Board's regulations.

If the pharmacy knows the lot number for the drug, it should place it on the label so that it can be returned in the event of a manufacturer's recall. If the lot number is unknown, the drug must be removed from stock and returned to the manufacturer or disposed of in the event that there is a recall of the drug.

** The medication cannot be returned to the stock bottle. **

What is a "device?"

A device is an instrument, apparatus, or contrivance, including their components, parts, and accessories, that is intended for use in the diagnosis, cure, mitigation, treatment, or prevention of disease in man or animals or to affect the structure or any function of the body of man or animals.

Can a pharmacy accept the return of medical devices for resale?

Yes, provided the device is in the manufacturer's original sealed packaging.

Drug Distribution

Can a pharmacy ever act as a wholesale distributor of small quantities of prescription drugs without being a licensed wholesaler?

Yes. Wholesale controlled substances sales can't exceed 5% of the pharmacy's total CII-CV annual sales in dosage units.

Example: if your pharmacy dispenses 100,000 dosage units of CII-CV drugs in a year, it can sell up to 5,000 dosage units that year without being licensed as a wholesaler. The 5% is based on total dosage units and is not tied to any one specific drug. Wholesale oxygen sales cannot exceed 5% of total oxygen sales.

Can a prescriber issue a prescription for controlled substances to stock/restock his office?

No. Prescriptions are only for patients. The doctor can order medications for his office using either an appropriate order form or invoice. The content of an invoice/order form will be covered in the recordkeeping section of this text. A DEA Form 222 is required if the medication is a CII drug.

What if the drugs to be transferred to another entity are CII drugs?

A DEA 222 must be used. The pharmacy will be the supplier so the party receiving the drugs must complete the DEA 222 and submit it to the pharmacy.

DEA Form 222 and Schedule II Drug Transfers

How do registrants get their initial DEA 222 forms?

The forms are given to registrants by the DEA when they are first registered if requested on the application form.

How do registrants get additional DEA 222 forms?

The DEA 222a form is used to order subsequent DEA 222 forms

What information must be included on the DEA 222a forms?

- Registrant's name
- Registrant's address
- Registrant's DEA number

- The number of forms requested (the books come in quantities of 7 or 14)
- The signature of the registrant or someone who has received power of attorney.

Registrants can also order new DEA 222 forms online at: www.DEAdiversion.usdoj.gov

Is a registrant allowed to delegate the ordering of DEA 222 forms and CII drugs to other persons?

Yes, the registrant can give power of attorney to one or more agents. The power of attorney must be retained in the files with the executed DEA 222 forms. The power of attorney can be revoked at any time be execution of a notice of revocation.

Is the pharmacy allowed to store or execute blank (unexecuted) DEA 222 forms at an address other than the one on the form?

Yes, but must the forms must be promptly provided to the registered location if it is being inspected.

Who fills out the DEA 222 form, the purchaser or the supplier?

The purchaser. The pharmacy fills out the form when purchasing drugs.

What if the pharmacy is returning drugs to a distributor?

The pharmacy will let the distributor know what CII drugs the pharmacy is returning and the distributor will fill out one of its DEA 222 forms and send it to the pharmacy.

What if a doctor or different pharmacy is ordering CII drugs from a pharmacy?

The doctor or receiving pharmacy would have to complete its DEA 222 form and send it to the distributing pharmacy.

What information is pre-printed on DEA 222 Forms when they are received by the pharmacy?

- The date it was issued
- The registrant's DEA number
- The registrant's name

- The registrant's address
- The Schedules, CI, CII, or both, that the registrant is allowed to order
- The registrant's business (e.g. retail pharmacy, wholesaler, etc.)
- The DEA 222 Form's serial number (each one has its own number)

What information does the purchaser complete on the DEA form 222?

- The name of the supplier
- The address of the supplier
- The date the form is completed
- The number of packages for each drug ordered
- The size package for each drug ordered (e.g. 100 tabs or 10 mL)
- The name of each drug order (e.g. morphine inj. 10mg/mL)
- The last line completed
- Signature of the person completing the DEA 222

The DEA 222 is a triplicate document. Where do the three copies of a DEA 222 go when drugs are purchased?

The purchaser fills out the form (in triplicate), and keeps Copy 3.

Copies 1 & 2 are sent to the supplier.

After the order is filled, the supplier completes Copies 1 and 2. The supplier keeps Copy 1 and sends Copy 2 to the DEA Special Agent in Charge.

What information does the purchaser add to Copy 3 of the DEA 222 when the order is received?

- The number of packages received in the packages shipped column on the form.
- The date each package was received in the "date shipped" column on the form.

What information does the supplier add to Copies 1 and 2 of the DEA 222 when the order is shipped?

- The NDC of each drug

- The number of packages shipped of each drug
- The date each package is shipped

How long is a completed DEA 222 valid?

The supplier has 60 days from when it is executed to fill the order.

If a supplier is unable to fill all or part of an order, what can the supplier do with the DEA 222?

The supplier can partially fill the order and provide the balance in additional shipments during the 60-day validity of the DEA Form 222.

How soon does Copy 2 need to be received by the DEA?

By the close of the month in which the shipment was filled.

If the order was filled in partial shipments, the close of the month in which the last shipment was sent or when the 60-day validity period expires.

When is a supplier prohibited from filling an order written on a DEA 222?

When the DEA 222 is:

- Incomplete
- Illegible
- Not properly prepared, executed, or endorsed
- Altered
- Erased; or
- Has a change in the drug's description.

What will the supplier do if it refuses to fill a DEA 222 order?

The supplier will return Copies 1 & 2 of the DEA 222 to the purchaser with a statement of the reason for refusal.

What must the pharmacy do with the rejected DEA 222?

The pharmacy is required to retain all 3 copies of the DEA 222 together plus the statement from the purchaser in their files. The DEA 222 cannot be reused.

Which copies of DEA Form 222 are the purchaser and supplier responsible for retaining and for how long?

- Copy 1 – kept by the supplier for 2 years
- Copy 2 – kept by DEA
- Copy 3 – kept by the purchaser for 2 years
- Unaccepted or defective forms – kept by the purchaser for 2 years along with the statement of the reason for rejection.

Where are the executed Copy 3 of the DEA 222 forms kept?

At the location printed on the form. CII records must be filed separately from CIII-VI records!

What if a DEA Form 222 is lost in the mail?

The purchaser executes another form, attaches a statement with the serial number and date of the lost form, and a statement that the drugs were not received.

The purchaser keeps Copy 3 of the lost form, Copy 3 of the new form, and a copy of the statement.

The supplier gets Copies 1 & 2 of the new form and the statement and fills the order as usual.

***If the supplier eventually gets the lost form, they must mark it "Not Accepted" and return it to the purchaser. The purchaser will attached copies 1 & 2 of the "lost" form to Copy 3 of the form and the statement. This creates the necessary record of what happened. ***

What if a DEA Form 222 is lost or stolen (but not lost in the mail)?

Upon discovery of the loss, it must be immediately reported to the special agent in charge of the DEA divisional office for that area. The report must include the serial number of each form lost or stolen.

If an entire book (7 or 14 forms) is lost or stolen and the pharmacist does not know the serial numbers of the forms, he reports the date the forms where issued or an approximate date if he does not know the exact date.

If the form(s) are subsequently located, this must be immediately reported to the special agent in charge.

Is a DEA 222 form required to transfer CII drugs from a central fill pharmacy to a retail pharmacy?

No.

Is a DEA 222 form required to dispense CII drugs to a patient pursuant to a prescription?

No.

What are the special rules for the Defense Supply Center of the Defense Logistics Agency?

They may get partial shipments at different times, to locations other than the location printed on the DEA 222, for a period of 6 months from date of the order. They must be buying drugs for delivery to armed services establishments within the United States.

Drug Disposal/Destruction

How may a pharmacy legally dispose of Federal controlled substances?

Request assistance from the Special Agent in Charge by submitting three copies of a DEA Form 41. The Special Agent in Charge may authorized the pharmacy to dispose of the drugs by:

- Transfer to another registrant authorized to possess the substance
- Delivery of the drugs to the DEA
- Destruction of the drugs in the presence of a DEA agent or other authorized person
- In such other manner as the DEA agent deems will not result in the diversion of controlled substances.

Federal law also allows Federal controlled substances to be disposed of in accordance with the procedures set forth in a state's statutes and regulations.

How can a Virginia pharmacy legally dispose of controlled substances?

The drugs can be transferred to any of the following provided the entity has a valid DEA registration (for CII-CV drugs):

- Manufacturer
- Wholesaler

- Practitioner (e.g. doctor or osteopath)
- Another pharmacy
- Any other person, or entity that is authorized to possess (DEA registrant) or provide for the disposal of the drugs.

Remember, any transfer of CI or CII drugs must be done using a completed DEA Form 222.

The pharmacy may also destroy the drugs by burning in an incinerator or other Board of approved method in accordance with the following procedures:

- Give the Board at least 14 days prior written notice
- The notice must contain the date, time and manner of destruction and the names of the pharmacists who will witness the destruction.
- What if the destruction date is changed or the destruction does not occur? 18VAC110-20-210
- The Board must be notified and a new notice provided at least 14 days prior to the new date of destruction.

Who must witness the destruction?

The PIC and another pharmacist not employed by the pharmacy.

What records of the drug destruction is the pharmacy required to keep and for how long?

The pharmacy must maintain a completed DEA 41 drug destruction form as a record of the destruction. The form must be kept for 2 years and retained in the pharmacy with its inventory records.

What information must be included on the DEA Form 41?

- Date
- Kind and quantity of drugs
- Signature of PIC
- Signature of the non-employee pharmacist witness

How may a pharmacy that is going out of business dispose of its stock of drugs?

The drugs may be transferred to:

- Another pharmacy
- A practitioner authorized to possess them (DEA registrant)
- A licensed manufacturer or wholesaler

Inventory & Recordkeeping Requirements

Pharmacy law includes substantial inventory and recordkeeping requirements. It is through the use of inventories and mandated recordkeeping that the Board of Pharmacy, DEA, and other regulatory agencies are able to ensure that controlled substances are remaining within the closed system of distribution created by the Federal Controlled Substance Act and that the licensee is complying with the multitude of pharmacy laws and regulations. Maintaining the required records is part of the practice of pharmacy and pharmacists can be sanctioned for failure to comply with inventory and recordkeeping requirements even if the failure was due to oversight, incompetence or mere negligence.

Inventories

When is a pharmacy required to take an inventory of its Federal controlled substances (CI-CV drugs)?

- Prior to opening on its first day of business (initial inventory)
- At least every 2 years after it's last full inventory (biennial inventory)
- When there is a new PIC, before opening for business that day
- When there is a theft or loss of CI-CV drugs and what was taken is not known
- When the pharmacy closes or transfers its business

It would be very unusual for a pharmacy to have CI drugs in stock because they do not have a medically accepted use. Therefore, inventories are generally done of CII-CV medications.

Are pharmacies required to inventory their stocks of CVI medications?

No.

When a new pharmacy opens for business, what are the initial inventory requirements?

There must be a complete inventory of CI-CV drugs before opening on the FIRST day of business. If there are no Federal controlled substances on hand, that fact must be recorded as the initial inventory.

If a pharmacy fails to complete its initial inventory for 3 days, how many separate offenses does this constitute?

Three.

After the initial inventory, how often does a pharmacy need to inventory its CI-V drugs?

Biennially (every 2 years).

The pharmacy completed its initial inventory when it opened for business on January 15, 2015. There is a theft of Federal controlled substances from the pharmacy in December of 2016, almost 2 years later. The pharmacy did not know what what taken and did a complete inventory on December 15, 2016. Does the pharmacy still have to take a biennial inventory two weeks later in January?

No. As long as a full inventory (e.g. theft or change of PIC) of CI-CV drugs is taken within 2 years of the initial or last biennial inventory, it can serve as the new biennial inventory.

Can the inventory be taken orally using a recording device?

Yes as long as the inventory is promptly reduced to writing.

What information is required to be on the inventory?

- Date of the inventory
- Time of the inventory; before opening, after closing, before or after shipment/distribution for a 24 hour pharmacy
- For each drug in finished form: Drug name, dosage form (e.g., capsule, tablet, suspension), quantity (use milliliters for liquids), number of commercial containers (e.g., 3 bottles of 500)
- Signature of the person taking the inventory

If the pharmacy is open 24 hours a day, what additional information

must be included on the inventory record?

Whether the receipt or distribution of drugs on the inventory date occurred before or after the inventory was taken.

If the pharmacy is NOT open 24 hours a day, the inventory must include what additional information?

Whether the inventory was taken before the pharmacy opened or after the pharmacy closed on the date of the inventory.

When there is a change in PIC, what are the inventory requirements for the outgoing PIC?

The outgoing PIC is not required to take an inventory but must be provided an opportunity to take a complete inventory of CI-CV drugs unless their is good cause to deny him this opportunity (e.g. he is charged with diversion).

Practice tip: if you are an outgoing PIC, take an inventory and keep a copy for yourself.

When there is a change in PIC, what are the inventory requirements for the new PIC?

She must take a complete inventory of all CI-V drugs on the date she becomes PIC. This must be taken prior to opening for business.

How long must inventory records be kept?

A minimum of 2 years.

How are inventory records filed?

Chronologically. And, the CI-CII inventory records have to be filed separately from the CIII-CV inventories. CIII-CV inventory records can be filed with CVI records.

Where is the pharmacy required to keep its inventory records?

At the site where the stock of drugs inventoried are maintained.

Are there any special requirements for CII inventories?

Yes. You must maintain a perpetual (ongoing) inventory of your CII drugs and reconcile the CII inventory (account for discrepancies) every 30 days. Electronic records are acceptable, but discrepancy reports must be reviewed at least once a month.

A pharmacy's CI and CII drugs must still be inventoried by an incoming PIC, in the event of a theft or loss, and along with the biennial inventory.

Do you have to count every single CI-CII tablet when you do an inventory?

Yes. You must do an exact count of your CI and CII drugs but you do not have to open unopened bottles.

Do you have to do an exact count of CIII-CV drugs?

No. You are allowed to do an estimated count of your opened containers as long as the bottle size is less than 1,000 tablets. You do not have to open unopened bottles.

Does the pharmacy need to maintain CI and CII inventories and records separate from other records?

Yes.

Can CVI inventories and records be maintained with CIII-V inventories and records?

Yes. CVI records may be kept separately or with CIII-V drugs but not with the other pharmacy records. The CIII-CV records must be readily retrievable.

Prescription Recordkeeping

Is the pharmacy required to keep hard copies of prescriptions on site at the pharmacy?

Yes. For CVI prescriptions, an electronic image is sufficient if it is legible and can be made available within 48 hours.

What about electronic prescriptions?

The pharmacy does not need a hard copy if the prescription was an electronic automated transmission from the prescriber. In that case, the automated transmission serves as the hard copy and must be maintained for no less than 2 years.

What about oral prescriptions?

Oral prescriptions need to be reduced to writing and maintained for 2 years. They must also be filed chronologically.

What information does the individual pharmacist have to record when dispensing a prescription?

The date of dispensing, and the dispensing pharmacist's initials. Electronic records are acceptable. If manual records are used, the information must be placed on the back of the prescription. The failure to indicate the quantity dispensed will result in the presumption that the entire quantity ordered was dispensed.

Can all prescriptions be filed together?

No. CII prescriptions must be stored separately.

Can the pharmacy file CIII-CV prescriptions with the CVI prescriptions?

Yes, but the CIII-V prescriptions need to be "readily retrievable." There are two ways to accomplish this:

- Stamp a red letter C at least 1 inch high in the lower right corner of each CIII-CV prescription, OR
- Use an electronic data processing system that allows identification by prescription number and retrieval of original documents by prescriber's name, patient's name, drug dispensed, and date filled.

How long does a pharmacy have to maintain the hard copies of prescriptions?

2 years.

Additional Recordkeeping

What must be in a pharmacy's record of receipt of CI-CV drugs?

- Date of receipt
- Name and address of the supplier
- The kind of drug received (e.g. oxycodone IR 5 mg tablets)
- The quantity of drug received

- The signature of the pharmacist receiving the order

How long is a pharmacy required to keep records of CII drug transfers?

The copies (DEA 222 copy 3) must be maintained separately from other records and be available for inspection for 2 years at the site where the drugs were received. The invoices for the CII medications received can be maintained with the completed DEA Form 222s and must also be kept for 2 years.

Can the pharmacy store executed DEA 222 order forms, inventories, and prescriptions for CII-CV drugs at an offsite location?

No!

What about other CII-CV documents such as invoices?

They can be stored off site if authorized by the DEA provided they are made available for audit or inspection within 48 hours of request.

In what order must the records be stored?

Chronologically.

The pharmacy has to keep a record for 2 years showing which drugs were dispensed, in what quantity, and the name and address of the person who received the drugs (this information is recorded on the prescription). Do any other entity's need to keep similar records?

Yes, anyone who sells, administers, or dispenses, or otherwise disposes of drugs needs to keep this type of record. For example, a record must be kept when a nurse administers a dose of lorazepam in a hospital. These records are kept 2 years.

How long must a pharmacy computer system be able to store information?

The system needs to maintain the information from the previous two years.

A pharmacy keeps its prescription records in an automated data processing system. Is the pharmacy required to print anything out?

Yes, the pharmacy must make a daily printout summarizing all transactions that occurred during the day. The printout is signed by each pharmacist who dispensed prescriptions that day to certify that the transactions were correct and assume responsibility for them. The pharmacy can choose to maintain a logbook instead and the pharmacists would sign it every day as certification for the prescriptions.

How are chart orders filed?

Chronologically

Chart orders may be filed using another method if:

- Dispensing data can be produced showing a complete audit trail for any requested drug for a specified time period
- Chart orders are readily retrievable upon request
- The filing method is clearly documented in a current policy and procedure manual

How is a chart order filed if it contains both an order for a CII drug and orders for drugs in other schedules?

If the drug is floor stock, no additional filing is necessary.

If the drug is dispensed from the pharmacy, the original order is filed with records of CII drugs and a copy of the order is placed in the file for the other schedules.

A log book may be used in place of a printout.

How long do pharmacies have to keep records of bulk reconstitution, bulk compounding or repackaging of drugs?

One year or until expiration, whichever is greater.

What do these records need to contain?

- Date repackaged
- Drug name & strength, if applicable
- Quantity prepared
- Assigned lot or control number (by pharmacy)
- Manufacturer or distributor's name and lot/control number
- Expiration date
- Pharmacist's initials

Pharmacy Inspections

What governmental entities have the authority to inspect a Virginia pharmacy?
- The Virginia Board of Pharmacy and its agents
- The Virginia State Police Drug Diversion Unit and its officers
- The Agents of the Drug Enforcement Administration
- The Inspectors of the Federal Food & Drug Administration

What entity has the broadest inspection powers?

The Board of Pharmacy. Its agents can enter and inspect a Virginia pharmacy any time it is open and they do not need a warrant or probable cause.

Can the Federal Food & Drug Administration (FDA) inspectors inspect whenever they want?

Yes, if they think there is a reason to inspect. They do not need an administrative inspection warrant. The FDA's inspection authority comes from its responsibility to assure that drugs shipped in interstate commerce are safe, effective, and properly labeled.

Do the FDA inspectors need to provide notice prior to an inspection?

Yes, for each inspection (but not for each entry during an inspection).

Can the FDA inspectors inspect non-financial records of the pharmacy?

Yes. If you are required to keep the records, the FDA is authorized to inspect the records. Inspections must be conducted at reasonable times in a reasonable manner.

If a business is registered with the FDA to manufacture drugs or Class II or III medical devices, how often is it inspected?

Every 2 years.

What is the inspection authority of the Virginia State Police's Drug Diversion Unit?

The State Police's Drug Diversion Unit must be allowed to inspect a pharmacy's records during normal business hours but their authority is limited to records related to specific investigations. Unlike the Board of Pharmacy, they cannot come in and go through all of your prescription and drug records. Their review will be limited to the specific patients or prescribers whom they are investigating.

Can the State Police Drug Diversion officer view, copy and remove patient records?

Yes but only if the records are relevant to a specific investigation.

What are the requirements when a drug diversion officer removes an original record?

The officer must leave a receipt and provide a copy to the person maintaining the records within a reasonable time afterwards.

What are the requirements if the drug diversion officer copies the records onto "magnetic storage media"?

The officer must leave a duplicate with the person who maintains the records (e.g. the pharmacist).

Are Board and drug diversion officers allowed to obtain samples of any stock of a pharmacy's drugs?

Yes. They must leave a receipt that describes the sample taken.

Are any records off limits to the Board and drug diversion officers?

Yes. The drug diversion officers and the Board's agents cannot inspect:

- Financial data
- Sales data, other than shipment data
- Pricing data
- Personnel data
- Research data

Aside from pharmacy employees, who may be allowed access to copies of drug shipment records?

- Agents of the Board of Pharmacy
- Virginia State Police Drug Diversion Unit Investigators ("officers")

- DEA agents
- FDA inspectors

Can the Board collect samples of drugs, devices, and cosmetics for inspection?

Yes.

Which establishments may the Board enter and inspect?

A pharmacy, or any other place in Virginia where drugs, cosmetics or devices are manufactured, distributed, stored or dispensed.

When may an agent of the Board come to inspect?

During normal business hours.

Are the agents of the Board and State Police allowed to make copies of the pharmacy records they are allowed to inspect?

Yes!

What if an agent takes an original record of the pharmacy like a prescription?

He has to leave a receipt with the pharmacy and provide a copy of the record within a reasonable time.

When can the Drug Enforcement Administration ("DEA") and its agents inspect a pharmacy?

The general rule is that DEA agents need either an administrative inspection warrant or the pharmacy owner's written consent to inspect it.

Under what other circumstances can the DEA inspect a pharmacy? 21 CFR 1316.07

- The inspection is required prior to the DEA granting some kind of authorization (e.g. a license).
- The Constitution does not require a warrant.
- It is an emergency and there is not time to get a warrant.
- There is an imminent threat to public health and safety.
- The owner consents in writing.
- The inspection is of a conveyance (something being moved) and there is

reasonable cause for a warrant.

What does the DEA need to show a judge to receive an administrative inspection warrant?

Administrative probable cause. This is different from criminal probable cause. Administrative probable cause exists when the facility carries on a regulated function and has not been recently inspected.

How often are manufacturers of CI-II drugs inspected by the DEA?

Every year.

How often are distributors of CI drugs inspected by the DEA?

Every year.

How often are all other registrants inspected by the DEA? 21

As needed.

What are these entities prohibited from inspecting?

- Financial data
- Sales data other than shipment data
- Pricing data
- Personnel data (other than data as to qualification of technical and professional personnel), and
- Certain research data.

Prescription Drug Samples

What is a prescription drug sample?

A unit of a prescription drug that is not intended to be sold and is intended to promote the sale of the drug.

When can you sell, purchase, or trade a drug sample?

Never!

Who is allowed to possess prescription drug samples?

Prescribers and health system pharmacies. Most health system pharmacies avoid possessing drug samples because of the risk of inadvertently billing for a drug sample.

What is required for a drug company to distribute samples?

A written request from a prescriber and a written receipt for the samples provided. The prescriber may authorize the drugs to go to a hospital or pharmacy instead of his or her office. The manufacturer must keep the records for 3 years.

Can practitioners licensed to prescribe drugs possess and distribute manufacturers' prescription drug samples of such drugs?

Yes.

Are retail pharmacies allowed to possess prescription drug samples

No.

Robotic Systems

Can a hospital or long-term care facility use a robotic system? For example, a night technician might use a robot to automatically pull each patient's medications for the upcoming 24 hours, then deliver them to the patients' medication drawers.

Yes, this is permitted.

Does the robot violate the requirement that a pharmacist verify every prescription that leaves the pharmacy?

The Board waives that requirement when a robot is being used but pharmacists must do daily random checks of 5% of the medications that the robot selected.

What else do pharmacists need to verify? 18VAC110-20-420(A2)

- That all prescription orders entered into the computer are accurate
- That pharmacy technicians restock the robot accurately
- That unit-dosed drugs are packaged and labeled accurately
- That expired drugs are removed from the robot

What happens if the robot selects the wrong medication?

The pharmacy must report the error to the Board and a pharmacist must check 100% of all doses until the pharmacy provides the Board with documentation showing the error has been identified and fixed.

What if there is downtime of the robot?

The pharmacy must report it to the Board.

Are any other quality assurance measures required?

Yes, the pharmacy must maintain records listing:

- Any downtime, discrepancies, or errors
- The total number of doses packaged and total number of doses picked by the robot
- The number of doses checked when conducting the 5% check

These records may be stored off site or electronically as long as they are retrievable within 48 hours.

Prescription Monitoring Program ("PMP")

What schedules of drugs are covered by the Prescription Monitoring Program?

Schedules II through IV.

Can the Board of Pharmacy add a drug to the substances covered by the Prescription Monitoring Program by designating is as a "drug of concern?"

Yes.

When a pharmacist dispenses a drug covered by the Prescription Monitoring Program, what must be reported?

- The patient's name, address, and date of birth
- The drug and quantity dispensed
- The date of dispensing
- The prescriber and dispenser's identifier numbers
- The method of payment for the prescription

- Any other information required to comply with state and federal laws

How long does the pharmacist have to report the information?

It must be reported within 7 days of dispensing.

Are there any situations where a controlled substance can be dispensed without being reported to the Prescription Monitoring Program?

Yes, reporting is not required for:

- A pharmaceutical manufacturer dispensing drugs as part of an indigent patient program
- A physician dispensing to a patient in a bona fide medical emergency or when pharmaceutical services are not available
- Administration (as opposed to dispensing)
- Dispensing within a narcotic maintenance treatment program
- Dispensing to inpatients in hospitals, hospices, or nursing homes

Veterinarians dispensing to animals within the usual course of practice

Is data from the Prescription Monitoring Program protected?

Yes. Improper disclosure of this information is a Class I misdemeanor.

Can a pharmacist delegate access to the PMP to a registered technician?

Yes. Access to the PMP can be delegated to another person licensed, registered, or certified by a health regulatory board provided that the person is employed at the same facility and is under the direct supervision of the pharmacist.

Theft or Loss of Drugs

What must a pharmacy do when it discovers a theft or unusual loss of controlled substances?

- Immediately notify the Board (or when they open if the Board is closed)
- If the exact kind or quantity of drug lost is not known, do a complete inventory of all CI-V drugs

- Within 30 days of discovery of the loss, furnish the Board with a listing of the kind, quantity, and strength of the drugs lost.
- Notify the area Field Division office of the DEA in writing within 1 business day. (for theft or a "significant" loss)
- Complete and submit DEA form 106 to the DEA field division office.

How does a pharmacy determine if a loss is significant?

By considering the following factors:

- Quantity lost in relation to the business
- Specific drugs lost
- If the loss can be associated with an individual or a unique activity
- Whether there is a pattern or random series of losses
- Whether the drugs are likely to be diverted
- Evidence of the diversion potential for the missing drugs

What form will the pharmacy submit to the DEA that details the loss?

A completed DEA Form 106, Report of Theft or Loss of Controlled Substances.

What does the Board of Pharmacy require?

The pharmacy has to report what was taken. If the pharmacy does not know what was taken, it must do a complete inventory of its CI-CV drugs.

How long does the pharmacy have to provide the Board with the list of missing drugs and what information must it include?

The pharmacy has 30 days to provide the list of missing drugs to the Board and the list must include:

- The kind of each drug lost/stolen (e.g. oxycontin 40 mg tabs)
- The quantity and strength of each drug lost/stolen.

How long do records (DEA Form 106) of the loss need to be maintained?

2 years.

If controlled substances are lost or stolen while being transported by

a common contract carrier (such as UPS or FedEX) between a central fill pharmacy and a retail pharmacy, who is responsible for notifying the DEA?

Whichever pharmacy contracted with the contract carrier must notify the DEA and submit the completed DEA Form 106.

Maintenance, Detoxification and Treatment of Addiction

If a doctor has a DEA number, does this mean that he can prescribe controlled substances to maintain or detoxify an addicted patient?

No. Any doctor may use narcotics for pain control, but treating addiction requires special registration.

What drugs can an appropriately licensed physician prescribe to maintain or detoxify an addicted patient?

CIII – CV drugs that are specifically approved by the FDA for maintenance or detoxification. Examples include Subutex and Suboxone.

Can a DEA registered prescriber issue a CII prescription for use in the maintenance or detoxification of a patient?

No. CII prescriptions cannot be issued for maintenance or detoxification. Appropriately licensed practitioners may administer or dispense CII drugs directly to the patient but cannot prescribe CII drugs for these uses.

Are there special registration requirements for a practitioner who wants to prescribe CIII-CV drugs for maintenance or detoxification?

Yes. The doctor needs to receive a waiver under the Drug Addiction Treatment Act of 2000 (DATA 2000). The Substance Abuse and Mental Health Services Administration (SAMHSA) maintains a list of doctors authorized to prescribe buprenorphine. These doctors may prescribe using a DEA number that is the same as their usual DEA number, but with an X in place of the first letter. Prescriptions for Subutex and Suboxone must have the doctor's "X" DEA number on the prescription.

There is a good faith exception for practitioners who are not registered. They are required to write a notice on the prescription. A pharmacist should rarely, if ever, see a prescription with such a notice on it.

What registration is required for a doctor to use CII drugs to treat narcotic addiction?

To use CII drugs (e.g., methadone), the doctor must obtain separate registration from DEA as a narcotic treatment program and have a separate DEA number for this purpose. They still cannot write CII prescriptions for detoxification or maintenance.

If a prescriber has a DEA number, does this mean that he or she can prescribe controlled substances to treat patients addicted to narcotics?

The prescriber may use narcotics for pain control but cannot treat addiction without the special registration.

Can methadone (CII) be administered, dispensed, or prescribed by a narcotic treatment program?

Methadone can be administered and dispensed, but not prescribed. A pharmacist can fill a prescription for methadone if it is used for pain control, but not for the treatment of addiction.

When can a physician or authorized hospital staff administer or dispense narcotic drugs in the hospital for maintenance or detoxification?

When it is necessary as an adjunct to medical or surgical treatment of conditions other than addiction. An example would be an addicted patient who was involved in a motor vehicle accident in which he sustained major injuries. Under these circumstances, the patient may need to have his addiction maintained in the hospital so that he is able to recover from his injuries.

Hospital & Long-term Care Pharmacy

What are the additional responsibilities of the PIC of a hospital pharmacy?

- Establishing procedures for and assuring maintenance of the proper storage, security, and dispensing of all drugs used throughout the hospital
- Providing for reviews of drug therapy

Is the PIC of a hospital pharmacy required to attend meetings of the Pharmacy & Therapeutics (P&T) committee?

No, but most of them do.

Does the Board need to be notified if a hospital pharmacy is opening a satellite pharmacy on the hospital's premises?

Yes. The satellite will need to be inspected and have an appropriate alarm system. Drugs cannot be stocked in the satellite until after the inspection is completed and approval given.

The PIC is allowed to delegate the ordering and distribution of certain drugs to non-pharmacy personnel. What are these drugs?

- Large volume parenteral solutions that contain no active therapeutic drug other than electrolytes (e.g. normal saline; ½ normal saline with 20 meq of potassium, etc.)
- Irrigation solutions
- Contrast media
- Medical gases
- Sterile sealed surgical trays that may include a Schedule VI drug
- Blood components and derivatives and synthetic blood components and products that are classified as prescription drugs

What are the storage requirements for these products?

They must be in a locked location when authorized staff are not present.

Which medical gas must be locked up all the times even when authorized staff are present?

Nitrous oxide.

Is after-hours access to a hospital pharmacy's drugs allowed?

Yes, if the PIC authorizes it, a nurse may get emergency medications that are in a secured area outside of the pharmacy. The drugs must be in the manufacturer's original packaging or in units prepared and labeled by a pharmacist.

What records of the withdrawal of these medications by the nurse need to be maintained by the hospital pharmacy?

- The date of withdrawal
- The patient's name
- The drug's name, strength, dosage form, and dose prescribed
- The number of doses taken
- The nurse's signature

How long does the pharmacy have to maintain this record?

For one year.

Can drugs in the emergency room be left out in the open?

No. The drugs must be kept in an area where access is restricted to authorized persons.

Automated Dispensing Systems

Hospitals are allowed to use automated dispensing systems (e.g. Pyxis machines) under certain conditions. What are these conditions?

- The drugs must be under the pharmacy's control.
- The PIC must have established procedures for stocking, storage, security and accountability of the automated dispensing system.
- Medications are only removed from an automated dispensing cabinet pursuant to a valid order or prescription. A pharmacist has to verify most orders before the drug can be removed for administration to a patient.
- Drugs in the automated dispensing cabinet must be in their original sealed packaging or unit-dose containers packaged by the pharmacy.
- The automated dispensing system must be capable of producing a hard-copy record of the drugs distributed, including the identity of the patient and of the nurse who withrew the drug.
- Personnel are only able to to access the automated dispensing cabinet using a personal access code.
- Proper use of the automated dispensing cabinets is set forth in the pharmacy's policy and procedure manual.

Who is ultimately accountable for the drugs dispensed from an automated dispensing system?

The PIC. The actual filling and stocking can be delegated to another pharmacist or pharmacy technician as long as the individuals are employees of the facility who have been properly trained. If a pharmacist does it, the pharmacist is responsible. If a technician does it, the PIC is responsible. The PIC may require pharmacists to verify the actions of the technicians.

What are the monitoring requirements for automated drug dispensing systems?

- They must undergo a monthly audit.
- Their operation must be reviewed periodically.
- They must be inspected periodically.

When a technician removes drugs from the pharmacy to load into an automated dispensing device, what recordkeeping requirements apply?

A delivery record must be made that includes:

- Date
- Drug name, dosage form, strength and quantity
- The hospital unit where the device is located
- A unique identifier for the device receiving the drug
- The initials of the person loading the automated dispensing machine
- The initials of the pharmacist reviewing the transaction (verifies that the technician has the correct medications for the machine; e.g. amlodipine 5 mg vs. 10 mg)

What is the technician responsible for doing when he loads the automatic dispensing machine?

- Verify that the count of that drug in the automated dispensing device is correct
- Note any discrepancies on the dispensing record and report them to the PIC.

The technician is always responsible for correctly filling the machine.

Who performs auditing of the automated dispensing machines, and how often?

The PIC or someone the PIC designates must audit the machines monthly.

What record of the audit is required?

The audit must be initialed and dated by the pharmacist who conducted the review – or by a pharmacist if a technician conducted the review.

What is included in the audit?

- The count of all CII-V drugs dispensed from pharmacy is checked against the quantity loaded into the machines.
- The count of CII-CV drugs on hand is checked.
- A 24-hour sample of administration records from each device is checked for possible diversion by fraudulent charting.
- Medical records are checked to ensure a valid order exists for a random sample of doses recorded as administered.
- The records are checked for compliance with the pharmacy's written procedures.

What if a discrepancy is found during the monthly audit?

The discrepancy must be resolved by the PIC (or someone the PIC designates) within 72 hours of the time the discrepancy was discovered.

What if the discrepancy is a theft or an unusual loss of drugs?

It must be reported to the Board of Pharmacy.

Is any other monitoring required?

Yes, the devices must be inspected monthly. Inspection includes checking for:

- Proper storage
- Proper location of drugs within the device
- Expiration dates
- Security of drugs
- Validity of access codes

The machines do not need to be physically inspected if the system can track refrigerator/freezer temperatures, expiration dates, and uses technology such as barcoding to isolate and identify each drug within the device. In that case, the reports and alerts generated by the machine are sufficient to meet the requirements.

How long does the pharmacy need to maintain the automated dispensing machines audit and inspection records?

Two years.

Can the records be maintained electronically?

Yes, under the following conditions:

- The records can be readily retrieved upon request.
- The records are maintained in a read-only format which does not allow alteration.
- A log is maintained showing the dates of audit and review, including which machines were reviewed, the time period reviewed, and the initials of all reviewers.

Is a separate dispensing record required if the automated dispensing device is located in an emergency room?

A separate record is not required provided that:

- The automated record distinguishes dispensing from administration.
- The device records the identity of the physician who is doing the dispensing.

Practice tip: It is considered dispensing when patients are given drugs to take home with them from an emergency room. It is considered administration when a nurse or other licensed person gives the drug to the patient.

A pharmacy wants to supply a long term care facility with an automated dispensing machine. What are the DEA registration requirements?

The pharmacy needs to get a separate registration for each facility. If another pharmacy also wants to put an automated dispensing machine at the site, the second pharmacy needs their own DEA number for that site as well.

Does the long term care facility also need its own DEA registration?

No. But, it does need a controlled substance registration from the Board of Pharmacy.

Under what conditions can a nursing home have an automated dispensing machine?

The drugs are under the control of the pharmacy providing services to the nursing home.

The pharmacy has on-line communication with and control of the machine.

The nursing home has a controlled substances registration.

Are there any special rules for stocking CII-CV drugs in a nursing home's automated dispensing machine?

Yes. A nurse or other person authorized to remove drugs from that device must sign for the controlled substances when they are loaded. The records are kept by the pharmacy.

The doctor writes a medication order for a patient in a nursing home. Can the nurse take the drug out of the automated dispensing machine and administer it immediately?

No. A pharmacist has to review and approve the order (done electronically). This means that the PIC must ensure there is a pharmacist with on-line access to the system available at all times to review prescriptions.

What are the rules for security, monitoring, and auditing of automated dispensing machines in a nursing homes?

The rules are the same as in the hospital:

- The machines must be audited and inspected monthly.
- The PIC must resolve discrepancies within 72 hours.
- The drugs in the drawer must be counted when the drug is restocked.

Floor Stock

When an institutional (e.g. hospital) pharmacy distributes drugs as floor stock within the institution, what dispensing records are

required?

The records of administration are acceptable for drugs distributed as floor stock. These records are referred to as MARs, which stands for medication administration records.

What schedule drugs can the pharmacy supply as floor stock?

Any schedule but a receipt is required for all CII-CV medications.

What records does the pharmacy need to maintain for drugs supplied as floor stock?

No records are required for CVI drugs

For CII-V, the pharmacy needs:

- A delivery receipt – including the hospital unit receiving drug along with the signatures of the dispensing pharmacist and receiving nurse.
- A record of the disposition/administration of the medications must be returned to the pharmacy within three months of the drug's use.

Is a nurse's signature required when a technician places CII-CV drugs in an automated dispensing device?

No. The electronic capabilities of these systems create a sufficient record, which floor stock does not.

Is it sufficient for the pharmacy to create/receive these records and file them?

No! There are significant auditing requirements. The PIC or someone assigned by the PIC must periodically (e.g., monthly):

- Match returned records with dispensing receipts – to make sure they reconcile.
- Audit for completeness – records must include the patient name, dose, date/time of administration, signature/initials of person administering drug, and the date the record was returned.
- Verify that the inventory is correct – that additions and deductions from inventory are correctly calculated, and sums are correctly carried from one record to the next.
- Verify that doses documented on administration records are reflected in the medical record.

How should the records be filed and maintained?

- The records must be initialed and filed chronologically.
- They must be maintained for 2 years.
- CII-V records must be stored onsite at the pharmacy.
- CVI records may be stored off site if they can be retrieved within 48 hours.

A nurse returns a patient's medication administration record that shows both morphine (CII) and Ambien (CIV) administration to the same patient. Is this an acceptable record in light of the fact that Virginia requires CII records to be maintained separately from CIII-VI records?

It is acceptable provided that the CII drugs are listed in a separate section of the record. The record should be copied and the original placed with the pharmacy's CII records while the copy is placed with the other records.

Is a nursing unit in a hospital allowed to return drugs to the on-site pharmacy for reuse?

Yes.

Long Term Care Facilities

Can a pharmacy provide floor stock to a long term care facility?

Yes but only if the persons administering the medications at the facility are licensed to administer drugs.

What drugs can be provided to a long-term care facility as floor stock?

- Intravenous fluids
- Irrigation fluids
- Heparin flush kits
- Medicinal gases
- Sterile water
- Saline

- Prescription devices

Who decides what the long term care facility may have as floor stock?

The pharmacist, in consultation with the medical & nursing staff of the facility.

When a prescriber discontinues a drug for a patient living in a long-term care facility. What can the facility do with the discontinued drugs?

- The drugs may be returned to the pharmacy for destruction or donation to an indigent program.
- The facility can destroy the drugs at the facility (this procedure is not controlled by the Board of Pharmacy).

What recordkeeping requirements apply?

- The facility must have a record of destruction and a record of drugs returned to the pharmacy.
- The record of destruction must be signed and dated by the persons witnessing the destruction.
- Copies of the records must be kept for 2 years.
- The pharmacy serving the facility must receive a copy of the record(s) and maintain the records for 2 years.

How long does the facility have to return or destroy discontinued drugs?

Within 30 days of a drug being discontinued.

Drugs returned from a long-term care facility are going to be destroyed at the pharmacy. Who must witness the destruction?

The PIC and another pharmacy employee. The drugs may also be transferred to another pharmacy licensed to accept returns for destruction.

If the drugs are going to be destroyed at the long term care facility, who needs to witness the destruction?

The Director of Nursing. If there is no Director of Nursing, the destruction may be witnessed by the facility administrator and one other person. The other person can be a pharmacist providing pharmacy services to the facility or another facility employee authorized to administer medication.

After the drugs are destroyed, what records must be maintained?

The original record of destruction must be signed and dated by the people witnessing the destruction. The long-term care facility maintains this record for two years and the pharmacy maintains a copy of the record for two years.

Are unlicensed personnel allowed to administer medications?

This may be allowed at a long-term care facility.

Unit Dose Dispensing Systems

What is a "unit dose system?"

Multiple drugs placed in unit dose packaging dispensed in a single container (such as a medication bin) labeled with a patient's name. Directions for administration are not provided by the pharmacy and are obtained from the order or medication administration record.

What is a "unit dose container?"

A unit dose container holds a single dose of a drug that is not to be administered parenterally and is administered directly from the container.

What is a "unit dose package?"

A unit dose package contains a particular dose ordered for a patient.

What are the labeling requirements for unit dose containers?

- Drug name
- Drug strength
- Lot number
- Expiration date

***Remember the patient's name, location, and dosage are on the MAR.

When a drug cart is filled in a hospital, what records does the pharmacy need to maintain? 18 VAC 110-20-420

119

- Date of filling
- Cart location
- Initials of the person who filled it
- Initials of the verifying pharmacist

How long is the pharmacy required to maintain unit dose filling records?

One year.

Pharmacies that utilize a unit dose dispensing system must maintain a dispensing record. What form of records are acceptable for drugs dispensed to a specific patient's drug drawer?

A patient profile or medication card – the record of dispensing is entered at the time the drug drawer is filled.

An electronic "fill list" that lists drugs dispensed to patients' drug drawers.

How long do these records need to be maintained?

Two years for CII-V drugs.

When a pharmacy is providing unit dose systems to hospitals or long term care facilities, how many days of a patient's medication may be dispensed at one time?

If only licensed persons will be administering drugs to patients, a 7-day supply of solid oral dosage form drugs may be dispensed.

If any unlicensed persons administer the drugs, only a 72 hour supply of solid oral dosage form medications may be dispensed.

If unlicensed persons will be administering drugs within the long-term care facility, does the pharmacy have any additional responsibilities?

Yes. It must:

- Train the long term care facility staff how to use the unit dose system
- Provide a medication administration record that lists each drug to be administered with full dosage direction – no abbreviations
- Medications placed in unit dose drawer slots must be labeled or coded to indicate the time of administration

If a hospital or long-term care facility uses a unit dose dispensing system, can medications be stored outside of the pharmacy?

Yes, as long as the drugs are locked and secure.

How is a hospital or long-term care facility required to store drugs for an individual patient?

In an individual drug drawer or tray that is labeled with the patient's name and location. All unit dose drugs intended for internal use must be placed in the patient's individual drawer or tray unless special storage conditions are necessary.

If the nurse in a hospital would like to have a "backup dose" of a drug available for a specific patient, can the hospital pharmacy provide it?

Yes. Only one backup dose unit may be maintained in the patient's drug drawer along with the other drugs for that patient.

Can a pharmacy technician transcribe the prescriber's drug orders to a patient profile card, fill the medication carts, and perform other duties related to a unit dose distribution system?

Yes, provided these are done under the personal supervision of a pharmacist.

Compounding

How is compounding defined under Virginia law?

Compounding is the combining of two or more ingredients under any of the following circumstances:

- Pursuant to the receipt of a prescription
- In expectation of receiving a valid prescription based on observed prescribing practices
- For delivery to a practitioner for administration in the course of his professional practice
- For purposes of research, teaching, or chemical analysis

What is it called when a pharmacy is compounding medications

without a prescription, not in anticipation of the receipt of a prescription, medications that are copies of commercially available products, or for resale not pursuant to a prescription?

Manufacturing! And, it is illegal unless the pharmacy has a manufacturer's license and is approved by the FDA.

If a doctor, veterinarian, or dentist does combines a drug product with another ingredient in their office, is it considered compounding?

Yes

Is it considered compounding when a practitioner (or person supervised by them, such as a nurse) mixes, dilutes, or reconstitutes a drug for administration to a patient?

No.

Is the pharmacy required to put a beyond-use date on compounded products?

Yes, in accordance with USP-NF standards.

Can a pharmacy compound without a prescription in anticipation of receipt of prescriptions based on a routine, regularly observed prescribing pattern?

Yes.

What information needs to appear on a compounded product?

- The name and strength of the medication or a list of the active ingredients and strengths
- The quantity of the product
- The pharmacy's assigned control number that corresponds with the compounding record
- An appropriate beyond-use date

Can a pharmacy distribute compounded drugs for resale?

No. Not even to another pharmacy under common ownership.

There is an exception that allows veterinarians to dispense small quantities (72 hours) of pharmacy compounded medications for an animal for treatment in an emergency situation when timely access to a compounding pharmacy does not exist.

If a pharmacy delivers compounded drugs to a hospital or nursing home, is this considered the distribution of drugs for resale?

No. If the drugs are compounded pursuant to valid prescriptions, the pharmacy can deliver them to a nursing home or hospital.

Can the pharmacy provide compounded drugs to a practitioner?

Yes, for administration to patients in the course of their professional practice, either personally or under their direct and immediate supervision. The practitioner must be licensed to prescribe the drug.

What must appear on the label when a pharmacy provides a compounded drug to a practitioner?

- "For Administering in Prescriber Practice Location Only"
- The name and strength of the compounded medication or list of the active ingredients and strengths
- Quantity of the drug
- The pharmacy's control number
- An appropriate beyond-use date in accordance with USP-NF standards.

Do pharmacists have to do the compounding, or can a technician do it?

A technician may compound if a pharmacist supervises the process. The pharmacist must complete a final check to verify:

- Accuracy
- Correct ingredients
- Correct calculations
- Accurate and precise measurements
- Appropriate conditions and procedures
- Appearance of the final product

Can a pharmacy compound with ingredients that are not considered drug products?

Yes, in accordance with USP-NF standards.

If a drug has been withdrawn from the market by the FDA for safety reasons, can a pharmacist use the drug to compound?

Not usually. But if the compounding would be for a use outside of the scope of the recall, it may be permitted. For instance, a drug may be safe for topical use but not for internal use. A product may also have been recalled because of an issue with the manufacturing process but the drug itself is safe for use.

Is a pharmacy allowed to compound a product that is essentially a copy of a commercially available drug product?

Not regularly. However, it is permitted if:

- There is a change in the product ordered by the prescriber for an individual patient
- The product is unavailable from the manufacturer or supplier
- The pharmacist is mixing two or more commercially available products together regardless of whether the end product is a commercially available product

What records must be maintained for a product that compounded for an individual patient?

- Name and quantity of all components
- Date of the compounding and dispensing
- The prescription number or other identifier of the prescription order
- The total quantity of the finished product
- The signature or initials of the pharmacist or pharmacy technician performing the compounding.
- Signature or initials of the pharmacist responsible for supervising and verifying

When compounding in anticipation of the receipt of prescriptions, what must be recorded?

- The generic name of each component
- The manufacturer or brand name of each component
- The manufacturer's lot number and expiration date for each component

(if unknown, the source of the component)
- The pharmacy's assigned lot number, if subdivided
- The unit or package size and the number of units or packages prepared
- The beyond-use date
- The criteria used for establishing the beyond-use date must be available for inspection by the Board.

Does the pharmacy need to maintain a complete compounding formula listing all procedures, necessary equipment, necessary environmental considerations, and other factors in detail?

Yes, if the instructions are necessary to replicate a compounded product or where the compounding is difficult or complex and must be done by a certain process in order to ensure the integrity of the finished product.

Is any kind of quality assurance required for compounding?

Yes, the pharmacy must have a formal written quality assurance plan that describes how compounding is monitored and evaluated in compliance with USP-NF standards. This must include training of personnel involved, and initial and periodic competence assessment.

Is sterile compounding allowed at any pharmacy in Virginia?

Pharmacies that produce sterile products must notify the Board of Pharmacy. The Board maintains a list of pharmacies that compound sterile products.

Automated Dispensing Bins

Automated Dispensing Bins are used in retail pharmacies to automatically dispense drugs into prescription vials. They are also used in unit dose packaging systems to produce unit doses.

If a pharmacy uses automated dispensing devices in which drugs are removed from manufacturer's original packaging and placed in bulk bins, what records must be maintained?

A bin filling record that includes:
- Date of filling

- Drug name & strength, if applicable, and quantity prepared
- Manufacturer or distributor's name
- Manufacturer or distributors lot/control numbers and expiration dates
- Assigned lot number
- Expiration date in accordance with USP guidelines
- Pharmacist's initials

Can you put more than one lot into a bulk bin?
Yes.

If multiple lots are place in one bin at the same time, what is the expiration date?
The lot that expires first will be the expiration date for the entire bin.

How is the pharmacy required to label the bins?
So that they can be cross-referenced to the filling record to determine expiration dates and lot numbers.

For bins that can hold more than one lot, what procedure is required to ensure that drugs are in the drugs in the bin are always in date?
- The device must dispense the first lot before the second lot and the expiration date will be the date assigned to the first lot.
- Allow the bin to "run dry" (all product removed prior to filling) once every 60 days with a record made of the run dry dates.

What if there is a drug recall of one of the lots in a bin?
All drugs in the bin must be removed unless:
- The technology used can ensure that the recalled lot has cleared, or
- The bin was run dry (no drug left in it) after the recalled lot was added to it and a record was made of the run dry date.

Central Fill and Central Processing of Prescriptions

Is it legal in Virginia to outsource prescription processing to another

pharmacy?

Yes. This is called a central prescription processing pharmacy arrangement. The pharmacy that does the prescription processing is called the remote processor.

This is different from a central fill pharmacy.

What is central or remote prescription processing?

It is when a pharmacy outsources prescription processing functions to another Virginia pharmacy or a registered nonresident pharmacy.

Does the central or remote pharmacy processor dispense drugs?

No.

What activities can a central or remote pharmacy processor perform?

It can:

- Receive, interpret, analyze, or clarify prescriptions
- Enter prescription and patient data into a data processing system
- Transfer prescription information
- Perform a prospective drug review
- Obtain refill or generic substitution authorizations, or otherwise communicate with the prescriber concerning a patient's prescription
- Interpret clinical data for prior authorization for dispensing
- Perform therapeutic interventions
- Provide drug information or counseling concerning a patient's prescription to the patient or patient's agent

Is it legal to outsource prescription processing to an out of state pharmacy?

Yes.

What are the requirements for outsourcing prescription processing to a remote location?

- The two pharmacies must have the same owner or there must be a written contract, including scope of services between the pharmacies.
- The pharmacies must share a common electronic file or technology that

provides the information necessary for non-dispensing functions.
- The central or remote pharmacy must comply with Virginia's laws and regulations for the supervision of and duties restricted to pharmacy technicians.
- The pharmacy technicians must be registered in Virginia or possess credentials similar to those required in Virginia.
- A Virginia licensed pharmacist must perform an accuracy check of all processing done by the remote processor.
- Both locations must have a policy and procedure manual.
- Records of processing tasks and the people performing tasks, which functions as a "who did what where" record, must be available or retrievable for inspection.

What must be contained in the "who did what where" record?

For each prescription processed:
- Each individual processing task performed
- The identity of the person performing each task. This includes both pharmacists and technicians.
- The identity of the pharmacist who checked the task, if applicable.
- The location where each task was performed.

What are the requirements for maintaining the "who did what where" record?

- The record may be maintained separately by each pharmacy or in a common electronic file shared by the pharmacies.
- The primary dispensing pharmacy must be able to retrieve, at a minimum, the records for the previous two years and these records must be available for inspection by the Board.

What are the requirements for outsourcing prescription processing to an out of state pharmacy?

- Both pharmacies must follow Virginia law for supervision of technicians and activities restricted to pharmacists.
- Technicians must be certified in VA or possess "substantially equivalent"

credentials.
- A pharmacist licensed in Virginia must perform a final check for accuracy. This pharmacist can be at the remote pharmacy or the dispensing pharmacy.

Is a pharmacy required to notify patients if it outsources prescription processing?

Yes.

How is the pharmacy required to provide this notice?

- A one-time written notification or
- A sign posted in the pharmacy in a location that is readily visible to the public.

What does the notice have to include?

- The name of the pharmacy providing central or remote prescription processing
- If the pharmacy uses a network of pharmacies under common ownership, this must be disclosed.

What must be spelled out in the policy and procedure manual?

- The responsibilities of each pharmacy
- A list of the name, address, telephone numbers, and permit/registration numbers of all pharmacies involved in central or remote processing
- Procedures for protecting the confidentiality and integrity of patient information
- Procedures for ensuring that pharmacists performing prospective drug reviews have access to appropriate drug information resources
- Procedures for maintaining required records
- Procedures for complying with all applicable laws and regulations to include counseling
- Procedures for objectively and systematically monitoring and evaluating the quality of the program to resolve problems and improve services
- Procedures for annually reviewing the written policies and procedures for needed modifications and documenting such review.

If a pharmacy is performing remote prescription processing for a hospital or long-term care facility, what additional functions may it perform?

- It may act on clinical data (e.g. changing a dose)
- Provide drug information to the nursing or medical staff of the facility
- Authorize administration of drugs to patients by appropriate facility staff

Are pharmacists who participate in remote prescription order processing for hospitals and long term care facilities required to be licensed in Virginia?

Yes!

Can a pharmacist licensed in Virginia access her employer pharmacy's database from a remote location to process prescriptions?

Yes, as long as the pharmacy establishes controls to protect the privacy and security of confidential records.

If a hospital or long-term care facility outsources prescription processing, are the rules the same as for a central/remote processing pharmacy?

There is one exception. Any pharmacist participating in remote prescription processing must be licensed in Virginia.

Does a hospital or long-term care facility that outsources need a "who did what where" record?

Yes. It has to be available by prescription order or by patient name and must be maintained for two years.

What is a "central fill" pharmacy?

A pharmacy that delivers filled prescriptions to a retail pharmacy for dispensing to the patient.

How does the central fill pharmacy obtain the original prescription?

It is provided by the retail pharmacy.

What records does a retail pharmacy have to maintain for each central fill pharmacy it uses?

- The central fill pharmacy's name

- The central fill pharmacy's address
- The central fill pharmacy's DEA number

What records does a central fill pharmacy have to maintain for each retail pharmacy it services?

- The retail pharmacy's name
- The retail pharmacy's address
- The retail pharmacy's DEA number

Are the retail and central pharmacies required to verify each others' DEA registration?

Yes.

Do these record need to be made available to the DEA?

Yes, upon the DEA's request.

Are there any special requirements necessary to create a central fill pharmacy relationship?

Yes. The pharmacies must either have a common owner or have a written contract or agreement that specifies the services and responsibilities of each pharmacy and how the pharmacies will comply with applicable law.

Where must the written contract or agreement be maintained?

At both the central fill and the retail pharmacies.

Do the pharmacies need to have a policy and procedure manual?

Yes.

What is required to be in the policy and procedure manual?

How each pharmacy will comply with applicable law

How dispensing records will be maintained; including:

- Prescription records for refills
- Maintenance of hard copy prescriptions
- Access to prescription information
- Identification of the dispensing pharmacist
- Identification of the counseling pharmacist

- Provision of records to the Board, if requested
- How prescriptions will be tracking during the filling, dispensing, and delivery processes
- How the prescription labels will identify the pharmacies involved in the filling and dispensing processes
- How patient confidentiality will be protected
- How accuracy and accountability in the delivery process will be assured
- How prescriptions that are not picked up will be returned to the central fill pharmacy and recorded
- How patient consent for the dispensing and delivery processes will be obtained

Does a pharmacy need a special DEA registration to act as a central fill pharmacy?
No. The DEA registration is the same as for a retail pharmacy.

Stat Drug Boxes and Emergency Drug Kits

Name four situations where a pharmacy may provide drugs that leave the pharmacy but aren't for a specific patient.
- Drug kit for licensed Emergency Medical Services program (ambulance)
- Emergency drug kit (e.g., a crash cart in a hospital, or other facility where licensed practitioners administer drugs)
- Stat drug box (e.g., in a long term care facility, for situations where waiting for the first dose might endanger the patient.)
- Stat drug boxes and emergency drug kits may also be supplied for correctional facilities, or other facilities where licensed practitioners administer drugs.

Stat Drug Boxes

Can the pharmacy prepare an emergency drug kit for a facility (e.g., a

hospital crash cart)?

Yes, under the following conditions:

- Only licensed persons open the kit and administer the drugs
- Only drugs necessary for patient survival are kept in the kit
- Only drugs for injection or inhalation, or sublingual nitroglycerin, are kept in the kit

Who decides what drugs will be in an emergency drug kit for a facility?

The pharmacist, in consultation with the medical and nursing staff of the facility.

What are the requirements for sealing an emergency drug kit?

It must be sealed to preclude possible loss of the drug. Once the seal is broken, it must not be able to be resealed without detection. There are two kinds of acceptable seals:

Seals with a unique numeric or alphanumeric identifier. The pharmacy keeps records of seals currently used on kits it has provided.

A built in mechanism preventing resealing or relocking once opened. The pharmacy resets this mechanism.

What must a nurse do after she opens an emergency drug kit?

- Fill out the form inside the kit with the name of person opening the kit, the date, the time, the name and quantity of items used.
- Make sure any drug used from the kit is covered by a prescription, signed by the prescriber when legally required, within 72 hours.

Is a pharmacy allowed to provide an emergency drug kit to a long-term care facility?

Yes, but only if the persons administering the drugs are licensed to administer drugs.

Can a pharmacy provide a stat-drug box to a long-term care facility?

Yes, but drugs at the facility may only be administered by persons licensed to administer.

What kinds of drugs are permitted in a stat-drug box?

- If delaying therapy could result in harm to the patient, then the drug may be kept in a stat-drug box.
- Schedule II through V drugs may be kept in the box.
- At most, 20 solid dosage units of drugs in each schedule are allowed (20 CII's, 20 CIII's, etc.)
- Liquid dosage units may be substituted for solid, but a bulk bottle may not be used for multiple patients
- CVI drugs may be kept in the stat-drug box as well.

Who decides what is in the box?

The same people who decide what is in an emergency drug kit – the pharmacist in consultation with the medical and nursing staff of the facility.

What are the sealing requirements?

The requirements are the same as for an emergency drug kit.

When a nurse opens a stat drug box, what is she required to do?

- Fill out the form inside the kit with the name of person opening the kit, the date, time, name and quantity of items used.
- Make sure any drug used from the kit is covered by a prescription, signed by the prescriber when legally required, within 72 hours.
- Return the opened box to the pharmacy.

What additional records need to be kept for stat drug boxes?

A list of the contents of the box – attached to the box, and included in the facility's policy & procedure manual.

An expiration date – the earliest date that any drug in the box will expire

Can a pharmacy provide an emergency drug kit or a stat-drug box to a correctional facility?

Yes, if the facility employs one or more full-time physicians, registered nurses, licensed practical nurses, physician assistants or correctional health assistants.

EMT Boxes

Is a pharmacy allowed to provide a drug kit for a licensed emergency medical services (EMS) agency?

Yes, but it has to be sealed to preclude any possibility of loss of drugs.

Who orders and administers the. drugs from one of these drug kits?

- An authorized practitioner orders them (either orally or with a written standing order).
- An emergency medical technician (EMT) administers them.
- The practitioner signs the orders afterwards.
- If the practitioner refuses to sign the order, the operational medical director for the EMS agency must signs and returns the orders with the kit to the pharmacy within 7 days.

What should the EMT do with the kit after it has been opened?

Return it to the pharmacy for exchange.

Does the pharmacy have to keep a record of the EMT kits provided and drugs administered?

Yes, the pharmacy maintains a record of the drugs administered for two years just like any other prescription or order. A record of the kit exchange is maintained for one year.

Collaborative Practice Agreements

According to the guidelines published on the Virginia Board of Pharmacy's web site, collaborative practice agreements only constitute 1% of the exam!

However, as pharmacists' responsibilities continue to grow, this section is likely to expand also.

Collaborative Practice Agreements

What is a "collaborative agreement?"

It is a voluntary, written, or electronic arrangement between a pharmacist and his designated alternate pharmacists with a licensed practitioner of medicine, osteopathy, or podiatry, a physician's office, a licensed physician assistant or a licensed nurse practitioner that authorizes cooperative procedures with respect to the practitioner's patients.

What are collaborative procedures?

Procedures related to drug therapy treatment, laboratory tests, or medical devices under defined conditions or limitations for the purpose of improving patient outcomes.

Is a collaborative agreement required for the management of patients in an inpatient facility?

No!

What may a pharmacist be allowed to do under a collaborative practice agreement?

- Implement, modify, continue or discontinue drug therapy
- Order lab tests
- Other patient care management measures for monitoring or improving the outcomes of drug or device therapy

What are some of the limitations on collaborative agreements?

They may only be used for conditions that have protocols that are clinically accepted as the standard of care, or are approved by the Boards of Medicine and Pharmacy.

Is the agreement between one pharmacist and one prescriber?

No, the a pharmacist may designate other pharmacists (such as staff pharmacists) to participate in the agreement.

If an institution has a collaborative agreement with a pharmacist, are doctors employed by the institution required to participate?

No.

Is the patient's consent required?

Yes.

Are pharmacists allowed to participate in "kickbacks," fee-splitting,

or special charges in exchange for prescription orders?

Yes, but it must be fully disclosed in writing to the patient and any third party payor.

Are pharmacists allowed to interfere in a patient's right to choose a supplier of medication or cooperate with anyone in denying a patient the opportunity to select his supplier of prescribed medications?

No.

About the Authors

Alexis Willihnganz Long, PharmD. is a hospital pharmacist currently practicing at HealthSouth Rehabilitation Hospital in Aldie, VA. In her pre-pharmacy life, she lived in Berkeley, CA and worked as a technical writer, project manager, and network administrator. She currently lives in Reston, VA with her husband, two sons, and a chihuahua. Alexis would like to especially thank Erin Sherwood, Director of Pharmacy, and the wonderful staff of HealthSouth for their wisdom, friendship, humor, and support. She is also grateful to Annette Reichenbaugh, Karen Dunavant, and the fantastic team at the Reston Hospital Pharmacy for giving her a start as a health-system pharmacist. The greatest thanks go to her husband, Chris, the "honorary pharmacist," for his unfailing love and support.

Douglas A. Lipton, JD, BS Pharm. is Assistant Dean for Student Affairs at Shenandoah University's Bernard J. Dunn School of Pharmacy where he teaches the school's three (3) credit pharmacy law course. He is licensed to practice both law and pharmacy in the Commonwealth of Virginia. He has practiced pharmacy in community and hospital settings and has practiced law as an Assistant Commonwealth's Attorney, as in house counsel, and as an attorney in private practice. He would like to thank his wife and children for being so supportive during his work on this text. He would also like to thank Dr. C. Eugene White for cultivating his interest in pharmacy law and for exemplifying the role of student dean.

Made in the USA
Lexington, KY
29 May 2018